Nurturing Young
INNOVATORS

Cultivating Creativity in the Classroom, Home and Community

By Laura McLaughlin Taddei and Stephanie Smith Budhai

International Society for Technology in Education

PORTLAND, OREGON ■ ARLINGTON, VA

Nurturing Young Innovators
Cultivating Creativity in the Classroom, Home and Community
By Laura McLaughlin Taddei and Stephanie Smith Budhai
© 2017 International Society for Technology in Education

Editor: *Valerie Witte*
Copy Editor: *Kristin Ferraioli*
Proofreader: *Linda Laflamme*
Indexer: *Wendy Allex*
Book Design and Production: *Mayfly Design*
Cover Design: Eddie Ouellette

Library of Congress Cataloging-in-Publication Data available

First Edition
ISBN: 9781564843906 (paperback)
Ebook version available

Printed in the United States of America

ISTE® is a registered trademark of the International Society for Technology in Education.

About ISTE

The International Society for Technology in Education (ISTE) is the premier nonprofit organization serving educators and education leaders committed to empowering connected learners in a connected world. ISTE serves more than 100,000 education stakeholders throughout the world.

ISTE's innovative offerings include the ISTE Conference & Expo, one of the biggest, most comprehensive edtech events in the world—as well as the widely adopted ISTE Standards for learning, teaching and leading in the digital age and a robust suite of professional learning resources, including webinars, online courses, consulting services for schools and districts, books, and peer-reviewed journals and publications. Visit iste.org to learn more.

Join our community of passionate educators

ISTE members get free year-round professional development opportunities and discounts on ISTE resources and conference registration. Membership also connects you to a network of educators who can instantly help with advice and best practices.

Join or renew your ISTE membership today!

Visit iste.org/membership or call 800.336.5191.

About the Authors

Laura McLaughlin Taddei is an associate professor of education at Neumann University in Aston, Pennsylvania, and a professional development speaker in higher education and PK–12 settings. She is dedicated to teaching and modeling the use of innovation, creativity, critical thinking, communication, and collaboration both within the classroom setting and beyond.

Stephanie Smith Budhai is an associate professor and director of graduate education at Neumann University in Aston, Pennsylvania. She developed and oversees a state-approved program to prepare K–12 teachers to design, deliver, and assess learning in online modalities, and has published several books and articles about instructional technology. She serves as the Pennsylvania Association for Educational Communications and Technology southeast region treasurer.

Acknowledgments

Thank you to all the community members, educators, families, and students who freely shared their stories, ideas, and pictures with us to make this book more inclusive, collaborative, and interesting. Your stories motivated us to continue writing and made this book more relevant and diverse. We hope to stay connected with all of you, and we look forward to future collaborations and adding to the many ways we all nurture young innovators. Thank you for cultivating creativity in the home, school, and community:

Rene Atkinson, Pennsylvania
Shannon Brace, New Jersey
Jim Butt, Pennsylvania
Maria Cheeseman, Pennsylvania
MaryBeth Cheeseman, Pennsylvania
Meghan Czapka, Pennsylvania
Mary DePaul, Pennsylvania
Discovery Teachers, Pennsylvania
Nicole Draper, Delaware
Quibila Divine, Pennsylvania
Nicole Fantom, Pennsylvania
Casey Gallagher, Pennsylvania
Lori Griggs, Pennsylvania
Marcella Ilisco, Pennsylvania
Christine Jones, Pennsylvania
Rina Keller, Pennsylvania
Joy Kirr, Illinois
Loren Loomis, Pennsylvania
DeShawn Lowman, Delaware
Helene McKelvey McLaughlin,
    New Jersey

Alyssa Milano, Pennsylvania
Peg Mischler, Wisconsin
Nancy C. Moretti, Rhode Island
Robert Neri, Delaware
Diane O'Donnell, Pennsylvania
Beth O'Rourke, Pennsylvania
Gabrielle Poole, Pennsylvania
Michael and Marlee Porter, California
Cecily Ridgeway, Pennsylvania
Dr. Deborah Roberson, New Jersey
Mandy Schauerman, Pennsylvania
Christiana Skinner-Walker,
    Pennsylvania
John Sperduto, Pennsylvania
Carolyn Stillman, Pennsylvania
Gail Switzer, Pennsylvania
Bernadette Taddei, Pennsylvania
Laura Tebbens, Pennsylvania
Rashanha Tiller, Pennsylvania
Brenda Wilson, Pennsylvania

Thank you to all of our students and community members who signed permissions forms to allow us to use pictures of you or your children from our family and community events or pictures we took while in our class as we were making, creating, and inventing. We truly appreciate all of you, and we hope that you continue to nurture young innovators and cultivate creativity in your own classrooms, homes, and community:

Dana Bittetti

Morgan Brandenberger

Tracey Woodruff Brown

JaRon Burnett

Shamita Carrigan

Sarah Cominskie

Richard Cominskie

Meghan Czapka

Viola Davis

Lauren Estrada

Tammy Finsterbusch

Lori Griggs

Angela Guiliani

Justin Highlands

Sephora Houinsou

Lindsay Kern

Patrice Lamar-Bey

Helene McKelvey

Robert McLaughlin

Dorothy McLaughlin

Jacqueline Paxson

Gabrielle Poole

Michael Porter

Kiera Scarbrough

Carolyn Stillman

Laura Tebbens

Sarah Vadala

Contents

Contents

Foreword

As parents and educators, we have a tremendous responsibility to teach our children to be more creative. They must know how to generate and implement high-quality, novel ideas over and over again. Creativity is a lifelong skill applicable to every walk of life. Creative thinking can be used in every challenge we face. Without creative abilities, our children will be at the mercy of others and the vagaries of a harsh world.

Sadly, most people believe creativity cannot be taught. They believe you're either born creative or you're not. That simply isn't true. Creativity and innovation are skills that can be taught and learned as with any other skill. I should know. I've taught systematic creativity to college students, high schoolers, third graders, and even kids with cognitive disabilities such as Down Syndrome. It *can* be done.

But it takes a coordinated and dedicated collaboration between our schools, our families, and our communities. That is the aim of this book.

In my work with primary-school educators, I sense their frustration when it comes to teaching creative thinking. I believe they recognize the need for it. Yet our schools still fall well short of what is needed. They're missing the opportunity to embed creative thinking in the early school years when it matters most.

Why? They either lack available teaching time due to the focus on other topics more relevant to state testing requirements, or they lack the teaching resources and materials for their classrooms. This book solves both problems.

By spreading the responsibility as a collaborative effort between families and communities, educators now have the opportunity to carve creative thinking into their curricula. The authors also provide a clear roadmap for teachers on how to get children to think creatively, work creatively with others, and implement innovative ideas. There are no more excuses for not teaching creativity in our schools.

To the readers of this book, let me first thank and applaud you for taking up the challenge. I must warn you that you'll be met with a fair number of resistors and naysayers as I have throughout my long career. Don't let it defeat you. Instead, let it energize you for taking up a fight worth fighting. When you encounter resistance, remind people of the wise words from Harold R. McAlindon: "The world leaders in innovation and creativity will also be the world leaders in everything else."

Before you charge on to read this book, stop and think about why you teach. If you're like all teachers I know, you do so to leave a positive legacy in the form of your students. You want them to go on through life happily and well prepared to make a difference. In a very real way, your efforts to read this book and follow its guidance will enhance the legacy you leave and make the world a better place.

—Drew Boyd, Co-author of *Inside the Box:*
A Proven System of Creativity for Breakthrough Results

Introduction

The Importance of Creativity, Innovation, and Technology Integration in the Early Years

This book came about from multiple opportunities of working with teachers, administrators, and preservice teachers, and recognizing the importance of not only fostering innovation and creativity in young learners but engaging families and the communities in the process. The earlier we encourage children to think creatively and to innovate, the more natural this mindset will become. To effectively foster creativity and innovation in young learners, we need the support and buy-in of families and our communities. This book focuses primarily on students in kindergarten through fifth grade, although much of what we discuss can be applied to younger or older learners. We believe that creativity and innovation should begin at home, in early learning centers, and in our communities even before children enter kindergarten, which is why this connection between home, school, and the community is so applicable to this topic.

Both authors have experience working with young learners and their families as teachers, administrators, and now, teacher educators, and believe that the evidenced outcomes of encouraging innovation and creativity in older students tell us that young learners can benefit from such encouragement as well. This book provides ideas and resources for teachers to embed these concepts into early childhood curriculum. We further believe teachers learn best from one another; however, finding the time to collaborate can be challenging. We hope this book provides a forum for discussion and a convenient way to explore this topic and helps teachers to put the ideas to use in their own schools and/or classrooms. Within this book, we share experiences we have had working to support early learners, families, and communities to become innovators and creators. We also share the stories of others we have collected while writing this book.

The U.S. Department of Education and the U.S. Department of Health and Human Services (2016) published a policy on early learning and educational technology that stressed the importance of young children having adults in their lives who "are well-informed on how to use technology to support learning at various ages" as well as having "opportunities to learn, explore, play and communicate through a multitude of approaches, including the use of technology" (p. 4). In our book, we use the guiding principles within this policy to support our technology and family engagement suggestions and stories. The four principles to keep in mind as you read this book and nurture young learners are as follows:

- Guiding Principle #1: Technology—when used appropriately—can be a tool for learning.
- Guiding Principle #2: Technology should be used to increase access to learning opportunities for all children.
- Guiding Principle #3: Technology may be used to strengthen relationships among parents, families, early educators, and young children.
- Guiding Principle #4: Technology is more effective for learning when adults and peers interact or co-view with young children. (p. 7)

We refer to these guiding principles again in our conclusion to remind us to purposefully and intentionally integrate technology with the children and families we work with. The principles can help us to self-assess and improve learning through appropriate technology use and increased collaboration with families, schools, and communities. Our book provides many ways to use technology to make and strengthen these connections.

The ISTE Standards for Students (2016) and the ISTE Standards for Educators (2017) are used as guides and referenced throughout this book. We have aligned each chapter with one or more of the Student Standards and connected chapter content to the Educator Standards. These standards encompass the skills and mindsets we hope students learn and carry with them in our connected, digital world. Among the skills highlighted within the Student Standards are that students become innovative designers, creative communicators, global collaborators, knowledge constructors, and digital citizens. The Educator Standards we cover address how teachers can be leaders and learners; build community and positive relationships with families and the community; use technology to encourage making, creating, and innovating; demonstrate cultural competence; and use technology to provide students with alternative assessments to show competency and to reflect on their learning. These themes apply to this book's focus, which is to foster innovation and creativity while involving family and community.

When integrating technology into the classroom, we believe the greater focus should be on the learning, rather than the specific tool being used. We suggest certain tools only to serve as examples so that readers can immediately put the activities and ideas in this book to use. Technology is simply a tool that can be used throughout pedagogical practice to enhance student learning. Many school districts have technology initiatives that provide students and families with 24-7 learning opportunities in traditional, hybrid, blended, and fully online settings. We can have excellent technology initiatives, but if the technology is not appropriate or used effectively, the initiative may need to be adjusted or better supported. In some schools, students as young as prekindergarten are provided with devices to use in the classroom and at home. When technology is integrated in a developmentally appropriate way that enhances or redefines learning, it can be an effective tool for bridging home and school. Throughout this book, we provide multiple developmentally appropriate ways to use technology with early learners, families, and communities.

Innovation and Learning Skills

The P21 Framework for 21st Century Learning was developed to provide a guide for those working with students and has been "used by thousands of educators and hundreds of schools in the U.S. and abroad to put 21st century skills at the center of learning" (Partnership for 21st Century Learning [P21], 2016, p. 1). In this book, our focus is on the learning and innovation skills identified within the P21 Framework as essential for students to be prepared to live and work in our global and diverse society. According to P21 (2016), innovation and learning skills are what students need to set them apart and to be "prepared for increasingly complex life and work environments in today's world" (p. 2).

The P21 Framework for 21st Century Learning, and specifically, the subskills listed in the creativity and innovation section, provides an effective way to assess whether we as educators are encouraging creativity and innovation in young children (P21, 2016). The following three questions can be used to guide adults as they continue creating and innovating with young children:

- Are children thinking creatively?
- Are children working creatively with others?
- Are children implementing innovations?

Defining Terms

There are several terms that are ubiquitously used in education as well as throughout this book. Because some of these terms can often hold different meanings for different people, we are providing definitions of these terms and how we have used them throughout this book:

- **Creativity:** The P21 Framework definitions (2015) stated that thinking creatively means generating ideas, creating new ideas, and building on ideas through evaluation and refinement. In addition, working creatively with others is being able to communicate ideas effectively, be tolerant and aware of diverse perspectives, and embrace failure as an opportunity to learn.

- **Engagement:** Our definition of engagement in the context of education is based on the work of Schlechty (1994), who said students who are engaged exhibit three characteristics: (1) they are attracted to their work, (2) they persist in their work despite challenges and obstacles, and (3) they take visible delight in accomplishing their work.

- **Family:** The makeup of today's families is changing, and there are many types of adults who provide care for children beyond their biological parents. Throughout this book, we use the word "family" instead of "parents" to describe mothers, fathers, aunts, uncles, brothers, sisters, friends, and any adult charged with caring for specific students. Family provides a more inclusive term for those students who may not be cared for by their biological parents.

- **Innovation:** We use Pete Foley's definition of the innovation process:
  ". . .a great idea, executed brilliantly, and communicated in a way that is both intuitive and fully celebrates the magic of the initial concept. We need all of these parts to succeed. Innovative ideas can be big or small, but breakthrough or disruptive innovation is something that either creates a new category, or changes an existing one dramatically, and obsoletes the existing market leader. We can obsolete ourselves or someone else, and it can be "sexy," or address a basic human need—both the iPad and disposable diapers qualify for me. But it needs to either create a new market, or radically change an existing one." (as cited in Skillicorn, 2016, para. 6)

- **Makerspace:** A makerspace, in its simplest form, is a dedicated space with tools, equipment, and technology that individuals can use to create and collaborate on various projects (Schrock, 2014). Anyone can create a makerspace, and all are different and tailored to the individual needs and interests of the students in your school. The types of projects created at a makerspace are infinite as the purpose of the makerspace is to encourage creativity, providing students with opportunities to have hands-on experiences and be creators not consumers. Because many of the creations can be shared outside of the school setting with the use of technology, using makerspaces helps to redefine learning.

- **SAMR:** The SAMR (Substitution, Augmentation, Modification, Redefinition) Model developed by Puentedura (2009) provides teachers and administrators with a framework to use when examining their use of technology. The four stages of the model are explained in Table I.1:

Table I.1 Four Stages of the SAMR Model

SAMR Stage	Explanation
Substitution	Technology replaces a tool to carry out the same function (Budhai & Taddei, 2015, p. 3).
Augmentation	Technology contributes to a change in the learning environment to improve functionality of the learning experience (Budhai & Taddei, 2015, p. 3).
Modification	Technology causes a significant change to the learning environment (Budhai & Taddei, 2015, p. 3).
Redefinition	Technology redefines learning and results in innovative teaching and learning environments (Budhai & Taddei, 2015, p. 4).

- **Young Learners:** We define young learners as learners between the ages of 4 and 10. However, many of the activities in this book can be adapted for either younger or older children.

Features of This Book

The most unique feature of this book is that it provides authentic ideas on how to encourage innovation and creativity while engaging families and the community. In each chapter, we've included takeaways that can be immediately applied to support critical digital age skills in our youngest learners. We hope you can use some of the features of this book to take risks and try new things in your classroom that will nurture innovation and creativity in your students.

Each chapter contains the following features:

- **Examples from the Field:** When we were writing this book, we sent out a request to teachers, families, and community members to share ways they have nurtured young innovators. The stories we received are embedded throughout the chapters. We believe the best way to learn and gain ideas about how to encourage innovation and creativity is through communicating with those who are already doing it. We are so thankful to those who took the time to share their stories with us. If you have a story to share, please add to the survey we sent out (tinyurl.com/InnovationandCreativityISTE) and we can post it on our Nurturing Young Innovators wiki (https://nurturingyounginnovators .wikispaces.com).

- **Community Connections:** In this section, community members share tips and stories with us related to their work with young learners. We highlight these stories and stress the importance of connecting with community members to better serve children.

- **If Doing This . . .,Why Not Try This?:** Theodore Levitt (2002) has stated, "What is often lacking is not creativity in the idea-creating sense but innovation in the action-producing sense, i.e., putting ideas to work" (p. 2). Our goal in the "If Doing This . . ., Why Not Try This?" sections is to couple the learning thought process with the action/making stage and to provide a tool for thinking about current pedagogical practices, including what is currently working and how it can be taken to another level. Many teachers are already doing amazing, creative activities in their classrooms, but they may be afraid to try something new or do not have the time to think comprehensively about an idea. We hope this section provides new ideas and serves as a spark to go beyond the current.

- **Projects to Nurture Young Innovators:** These sample projects encourage innovation and creativity and are connected to national and Common Core State Standards. We provide ideas that we hope can be implemented right away. The projects can also be integrated into a teacher preparation program and completed by preservice teachers. We strongly believe that teachers need opportunities to take risks and innovate themselves so they can support their students to do the same.

- **Reflection Questions:** At the end of every chapter, we provide reflection questions that can be used individually by teachers to reflect on their own practices or as part of a learning community where group discussions take place. These questions can also be used as part of a teacher education program to help preservice teachers reflect as they prepare to teach young learners.

- **Checklists and Exercises:** We provide checklists and exercises throughout the book to help implement projects, support creative thinking, and suggest innovations that support young learners. According to Boyd and Goldenberg (2013) all innovations can be implemented by following five templates (p. 4–6). We expand this idea to apply to young children and families and how they can use these ideas to nurture young innovators. We created a wiki (nurturingyounginnovators. wikispaces.com) to share the exercise and checklist templates so that you can download and modify them for your own use. On our wiki, we will continue to share ideas with you even after you are finished reading this book, and we hope you can join and collaborate with us there.

Additional Resources: At the end of the book in Appendix A, we've included a Resources section listing websites, TED Talks, podcasts, Twitter hashtags, and other tools to help families, teachers, and communities continue to engage young learners in creative and innovative activities.

Suggestions for Using This Book

We wrote this book to provide resources for encouraging creativity and innovation in early learners while engaging families. The ideas can be implemented right away. Some of the topics we discuss include service-learning, project-based learning, makerspaces, and sharing learning with families and the community. The chapters may be read in any order, so, for example, if you need information on service-learning, you can go directly to Chapter 6 and start there. As stated earlier, the reflection questions found at the end of each chapter can be used for individual reflection, for classroom reflection as part of a teacher education course, or as part of a learning community within a school.

Incorporating Creativity, Innovation, and Technology Integration in the Early Years

"Around here, however, we don't look backwards for very long. We keep moving forward, opening up new doors and doing new things, because we're curious ... and curiosity keeps leading us down new paths."

—*Walt Disney Company*

Does everyone have the potential to be creative? Does everyone have the potential to be innovative? We believe the answer to both of these questions is yes. But after working with many adults over the years, we've found that when asked if they consider themselves creative, the answer is usually no. And if people don't think of themselves as creative, it is difficult for them to encourage creativity and innovation in others.

Children are naturally curious and open to learning, but as we reiterate throughout this book, they need the support of adults in their lives who understand this. According to the ISTE Standards for Educators, teachers are called to "establish a learning culture that promotes curiosity and critical examination of online resources and fosters digital literacy and media fluency" (International Society for Technology in Education [ISTE], 2017). In addition, teachers should "model and nurture creativity and creative expression to communicate ideas, knowledge or connections" (ISTE, 2017). Moreover, if we expect teachers and families to encourage creativity and innovation in young children, we need to provide them with tools to foster these skills through the application of "psychological safety, psychological freedom, and social support" (Isenberg & Jalongo, 2010, p. 17).

In this chapter, we provide practical suggestions to help teachers encourage creative thinking and innovation in young learners in the classroom, home, and community. In addition, we provide tips on how to engage families and the community in promoting these critical digital age skills and in empowering early learners to be lifelong learners.

Chapter Overview

This chapter will cover the following:

- Supporting students as digital citizens and innovative designers
- Providing teachers and parents opportunities to work collaboratively to support children's creativity
- Encouraging possibility thinking, and thinking both inside and outside of the box
- Developing a mindset toward purposeful technology integration for young learners
- Partnering with schools and community members to encourage innovation and creativity in young learners

Student as Digital Citizen and Innovative Designer

Throughout this book, we embed the ISTE Standards for Students to remind us all to help students learn these skills so they can become productive and capable digital learners. As indicated, "the standards are designed for use by educators across the curriculum, with every age student, with a goal of cultivating these skills throughout a student's academic career" (ISTE, 2016). We begin with the Student Standards for digital citizen and innovative designer.

Digital Citizen

"Students recognize the rights, responsibilities and opportunities of living, learning and working in an interconnected digital world, and they act and model in ways that are safe, legal and ethical."

— *ISTE Standards for Students, Standard 2: Digital Citizen*

Ensuring children's safety and teaching children to be responsible digital citizens are essential when integrating technology in the classroom and encouraging innovation. To be a digital citizen, it is important to have access to the internet and advocate for internet safety for all children. (We address issues surrounding developmental appropriateness of technology use with young children in the "Using Technology Purposefully" section later in this chapter.) Students must be able to use, manage, and navigate the digital world, without compromising who they are or their integrity. They must be aware of the implications of inappropriate technology use and how to engage in online forums. Even at a young age, students must understand how to show respect online, communicate effectively, and use information appropriately. They must learn what intellectual property is and know about fair use and other applicable laws. At a minimum, teachers should inform students and families about the following:

- Children's Internet Protection Act (goo.gl/bIWcOH)
- Fair Use Index (www.copyright.gov/fls/fl102.html)
- Library Services and Technology Act (www.ala.org/advocacy/advleg/federallegislation/lsta)
- Technology, Education and Copyright Harmonization ("TEACH") Act (S. 487) (https://copyright.gov/docs/regstat031301.html)

Digizen (digizen.org) is an excellent resource for families, schools, and children to use for increasing their awareness and understanding of digital citizenship. Technology use should be supervised and facilitated by a responsible adult who understands digital citizenship. In schools, teachers will provide that support. Figure 1.1 illustrates an example of a Digital Citizens bulletin board created to engage families on the importance of teaching children to be good digital citizens and using the resources from Common Sense Media (commonsensemedia.org). In the home, adult families will provide supervision of children's technology use. Community members, such as librarians, can serve in the role of ensuring students are using safe practices when they are using computers and the internet at local libraries.

Figure 1.1 This Digital Citizens bulletin board was created by Christine Jones and used to engage families on the importance of teaching children how to be good digital citizens. Photo credit: John Sperduto

The National Cyber Security Alliance (2017) has provided the following tips for developing good digital citizens on its website (https://StaySafeOnline.org):

- Remain aware and engaged in what children are doing online.
- Support good choices.
- Keep the computer clean of viruses, protected with antivirus software and updated.
- Use the safety features provided by most software and Internet Service Providers to help you protect children from harm—these include setting up pre-approved websites children can visit and allowing you to set limits on the time children spend online.
- Check and monitor the privacy settings on the software and devices children are using.
- Encourage critical thinking and teach children that good digital citizens respect the privacy of others; teach children not to share anything that would be embarrassing or hurtful to someone else.
- Act as digital citizen leaders by keeping the lines of communication open with children so they feel they can tell you if something is wrong. Also, encourage children to seek help if a friend is making unsafe choices.

Innovative Designer

"Students use a variety of technologies within a design process to identify and solve problems by creating new, useful or imaginative solutions."

— *ISTE Standards for Students, Standard 4: Innovative Designer*

Young children become innovative designers when they have opportunities to think creatively and to solve and think through open-ended problems. In this chapter, we discuss ways to provide these opportunities both through a design process and through open-ended activities and exploration. We also believe that in order for young learners to be innovative and creative, they need adults in their lives who are innovative designers.

Innovative, Who Me?

The more time we all provide our students to be creative and innovative, the more they will realize that everyone can be innovative. Yes, even you can be innovative. For example, woodworking has been used in early learning centers for many years. When young children are exposed to real materials and tools, like hammers, nails, and a saw, they can learn how to use them effectively. Of course, the children must be supervised and provided with direct instruction on how to use the tools safely. If adults have not had experience with this kind of activity, they may be hesitant to integrate it into their classroom or home environment.

As teacher educators, we have found the best way to teach our students how to nurture creativity and innovation with their own students is to give them hands-on opportunities to be creative and innovative. For this reason, we provided our students, who will be future teachers, with opportunities to collaborate, saw, hammer, and create in one of their methods courses.

Figure 1.2 Future teachers taking risks, doing woodworking, and creating together during their science methods course with Dr. Taddei. Photo credit: Meghan Czapka

The students used resources that were available to them and created a unique flower box (Figure 1.2). They had to come up with something to make from the materials they were provided and they were excited and engaged during the activity. Some of the students worked with materials and tools they had never used before, like a saw.

One of the top ten attributes employers look for in new college graduates is the ability to "be creative and innovative in solving problems" (Association of American Colleges and Universities, 2007). At the university where we teach, both our undergraduate and graduate teacher certification programs require a course in which teachers and future teachers have opportunities to integrate the arts. Within this course, we have found that if we want teachers to go out and foster creativity and innovation with the students they teach, they need hands-on opportunities to think and work creatively with others—and this approach has been shown to be effective for others, too.

For example, Nancy, who served as an administrator and worked with children for 28 years, shared an example of how she incorporated creative and innovative problem solving when working with young children:

> We had a "peace table." This center consisted of a tiny table where two children who were struggling to get along were asked to sit and play a game, share in a discussion, draw together, or just sit quietly. As they sat, I would jump in and out of their discussion or observe from a distance until I found them smiling and laughing with each other. This allowed children to become creative as they explored ideas for negotiation and ways to play collaboratively.

In contrast to this approach, often when students exhibit challenging behaviors, they are put in a corner or asked to remove themselves from the larger group. This can create an isolated experience and negatively impact a young child's self-esteem and school experience. Nancy's technique of using the "peace table" in the field demonstrates the ability of using tough times and behaviors to impact change, influence the job, and draw on the creativity and collaborative potential of children.

Cameron Herold's (2010) eye-opening TED Talk, "Let's Raise Kids to be Entrepreneurs" (goo.gl/gjqi1U), is another helpful example. Herold encourages adults to teach children how to lead others, how to learn from mistakes, how to ask for help when they need it, and to always look for solutions. Children have dreams and visions for their future, and many times you can help them identify their passions early on and support them in pursuing the interests that excite them most.

Possibility Thinking

The Centre for Research in Education and Educational Technology (n.d.) has described possibility thinking as "enabling the transition from 'what is' to 'what might be.' It involves a range of features: questioning, play, immersion, making connections, imagination, innovation, risk-taking and self-determination" (p. 3). With this in mind, we created a Possibility Thinking Card that can be used when working with young learners and encouraging possibility thinking (Figure 1.3). The Possibility Thinking Card is extremely flexible and can be applied to a variety of contexts and academic subjects.

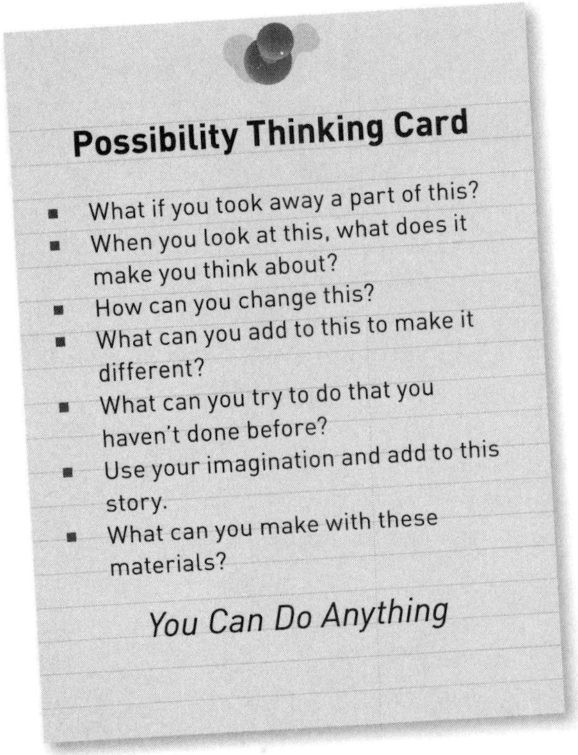

The goal of the Possibility Thinking Card is to go beyond what's there and imagine greater possibilities. The card requires students to use their creative and critical thinking skills to truly go beyond the norm. In today's world, it's critical to encourage children to think creatively at very young ages and to inspire them to have no limits to their ideas and what they are able to do. The Possibility Thinking Card encourages students

Possibility Thinking Card

- What if you took away a part of this?
- When you look at this, what does it make you think about?
- How can you change this?
- What can you add to this to make it different?
- What can you try to do that you haven't done before?
- Use your imagination and add to this story.
- What can you make with these materials?

You Can Do Anything

Figure 1.3 Possibility thinking encourages young learners to think creatively and become innovative designers. This Possibility Thinking Card can help children extend their thinking and imagination.

to not settle for their first ideas and to always build on what they have to make it more useful and expansive.

Questioning is an essential digital age skill and a requirement for being successful. The Possibility Thinking Card serves as a foundation for students in building a mindset for inquiry-based learning. Students can share their responses to the card with their peers and establish a learning community where their ideas can be further dissected, encouraged, and questioned.

Curiosity drives possibility thinking. As adults working with young learners, we need to find ways to cultivate curiosity. Hummell (2015) has provided the following tips for nurturing curiosity both at home and in school:

- Be aware of children's interests and plan activities related to their interests.
- Discuss and explore differing perspectives.
- Encourage curiosity and creativity.

The earlier children develop these important skills, the easier it will be for them to continue being creative, curious, and innovative in the later years.

Inside the Box: Systematic Inventive Thinking

Many times, we think of creativity and innovation as involving thinking outside the box. However, Boyd and Goldenberg (2013) have offered an interesting perspective on inside-the-box thinking. They believe that anyone can be creative and innovative by following one of five templates. These templates form the theory of Systematic Inventive Thinking (SIT) and include subtraction, division, multiplication, task unification, and attribute dependency. Table 1.1 shows ways to incorporate SIT while working with young innovators and making creativity an option for everyone. This inside-the-box thinking is described as "a way to create truly innovative ideas anytime using resources close at hand" (Boyd & Goldenberg, p. 9).

Table 1.1 Systematic Inventive Thinking (SIT)

Template	What Does It Mean?	Example
Subtraction	Eliminate or reduce something on a product	Small earbud headphones were developed by reducing the size of large over-the-ear headphones.
Multiplication	Taking a component and copying it	Boyd (2015) described a time when he was working with young children and he asked them to take an ordinary object, like an umbrella, and use the Multiplication feature of SIT. The children came up with the idea to create an umbrella with two handles—one where the handle would normally be and the other on top of the umbrella. Their idea was to have a handle available for the times when the wind blew the umbrella inside out.
Division	Divide the product or one of the components	Controls from a PWC were placed in the handle of a tow rope, which allowed the wakeboarder to control the boat without needing another person to pilot the boat. Boyd's "Inside the Box" blog (goo.gl/Oymdho) provides many examples of SIT.
Task Unification	Combining functions into an existing component	Instead of having a food storage container and a cup, an example of Task Unification is creating a food storage cup that serves both as a cup and as a way to store food.
Attribute Dependency	Creation or removal of functions between products	An example of Attribute Dependency provided by Boyd (2015) is a coat hanger that can be expanded different ways to fit the item it is used for.

Boyd (2015) introduced SIT to young children and gave them ordinary household objects (flashlight, coat hanger, watch, shoe, etc.) and asked them to come up with a new invention for the ordinary object of their choice while working through the SIT process. This strategy aligns with the Student Standard for innovative designer, which states students would "know and use a deliberate design process for generating ideas, testing theories, creating innovative artifacts or solving authentic problems" (ISTE, 2016). At the same time, the Educator Standards encourage

>> Exercise 1.1 Think Creatively

Write or draw a picture of an item you like to use below:

List or draw pictures of features that are included in this item you drew or wrote about:

What can you take away or add to this item to make it different?

Will this make the item better? Why or why not?

Draw a picture that shows the additions or subtractions to the item:

teachers to "create learning opportunities that challenge students to use a design process and/or computational thinking to innovate and solve problems" (ISTE, 2017). When children are given opportunities to think creatively, they will surprise you with their ideas. You can ask children to look around their world and find something they like to use and then think about the features of this item and how it interacts with other things. Like the everyday household items Boyd (2015) used, there are items in children's homes or also within the classroom that can be leveraged for a similar activity involving SIT and inquiry-based creative thinking.

Exercise 1.1 can be used to help young children think creatively by applying SIT. You can access the exercise template for download and use from the Resources page at tinyurl.com/NYL-thinkcreatively.

Exercise 1.2 can be used to help adults think through the design process using SIT.

❯❯ Exercise 1.2 Applying Systematic Inventive Thinking (SIT)

Things You Can Change (components, features, and functions)	Things You Can't Change (environmental factors—physical factors, social factors, etc.)	What Changes Could You Make? (Subtraction, Multiplication, Division, Task Unification, Attribute Dependency)	How Might These Changes Be Beneficial?

When considering the use of SIT with young learners, keep in mind that the more materials children have access to, the more opportunities they have to be creative and innovative. And even if you don't have access to many materials, you can create them. As many teachers know, lack of resources and materials can be an issue when teaching—so why not make use of resources already at your disposal? Doing so is also a good way to involve families and ask them to assist with providing resources they already have. For example, if you want your students to have opportunities to explore and take apart items in class, you can ask families to donate those items to the classroom.

Here is a list of possible items that could be used to accomplish the goal of exploring and taking apart (however, such a list can be endless, because opportunities for thinking creatively are everywhere):

Explore and Take Apart Items: Used/Found Items to Request from Families

- Old computers
- Old electronics (radio, alarm clock, toaster, etc.)
- Cell phones
- Handheld battery operated fans
- Umbrellas
- Cardboard boxes
- Tools (hammers, saws, pliers, screwdrivers, etc.)
- Dry wall
- PVC pipes
- Old shoes
- Used doorknobs
- Packing foam
- Old keys

When providing children with tools and items as mentioned in the previous list, it's always important to model how to use the tool or item safely and to also provide supervision. Boyle, Butler, and Li (2017) suggested, "an experience with an old rotary telephone is more likely to generate layered conversations about how technology actually worked to support human communication than the smartphone" (p. 51). These kinds of hands-on explorations provide a perfect opportunity to introduce science terms and concepts to students while they are engaged. For example, as they take apart these items, you can talk about simple machines and how they need certain components to run.

The idea of teaching children how to use SIT goes well with this activity because it requires asking children to think about the features of an item, what they can change about it, and how this could be beneficial. When children explore everyday household items, this can help them to think creatively and innovatively (Boyle, Butler, & Li, 2017). Providing young children with authentic learning experiences is critical in helping them to meet the student standard for innovator designer. The process of thinking through real-life problems and coming up with solutions for those problems fosters children's creativity and helps them learn how to problem solve, analyze, and communicate their thinking (Strimel, 2014), which are all components of the design process.

Thinking Outside the Box

Ideally, adults can support young children in having varied experiences and developing the ability to think outside the box and experiment with open-ended materials in their own ways. For example, Diane encourages outside-the-box thinking by using movement breaks to foster creativity in her students and to help them focus: "Depending on what group I am working with, I use movement breaks to help my students refocus. I also use various rewards to motivate students, such as rewarding with tickets or rewarding with time on Kindles."

Here are some suggestions for creating authentic learning experiences through outside-the-box thinking to nurture innovation and creativity:

Create Prop Boxes: A prop box is a box filled with a variety of props that can be used to encourage creative thinking and imaginative play in young children. These prop boxes can connect with real themes that are happening in the children's lives. For example, you could have a theme around visiting a veterinarian, moving to a new home, or running a restaurant. Listen to the children's interests and create prop boxes around their interests. Prop boxes can also be used to inspire future career readiness with themed boxes based on a particular career or profession.

Role Play: Have children use their creativity to reenact scenarios that you provide. For example, give students scenarios that involve conflict and problem resolution and help them think through the problems. Role play can also be used to model and provide students with practice of various skills, such as oral language skills and learning how to communicate needs.

Community Connections

Encouraging Innovation through Systematic Inventive Thinking

Jim Butt, Community Member, Aerospace Engineer

Jim partnered with his employer and the local school district to encourage innovation through Systematic Inventive Thinking (SIT). His company wanted to sponsor innovation within schools. As part of this initiative, employees were encouraged to collaborate with school districts and set up opportunities to talk to students about how to be innovative. Jim used SIT, discussed by Boyd and Goldenberg (2013), to help students think through ways to be creative. He visited K–12 classrooms within the district and talked with students and teachers about innovation.

Jim led innovation initiatives within his company and shared ways to be creative and innovate using design thinking. He found that anyone can be creative and innovative when using the steps of SIT. Also, Jim believed exposing children to SIT early on helps to nurture young innovators. He followed the work of Boyd and Goldenberg (2013), and created a graphic

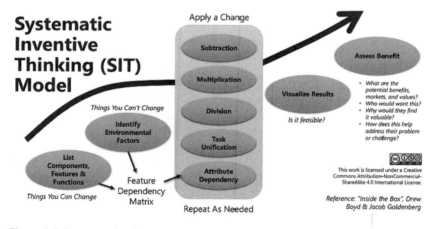

Figure 1.4 Jim created a visual explaining the SIT process. This design thinking process can be used to think through how a current object or idea can be changed. Photo credit: Jim Butt

(continued on next page)

[continued from previous page]

(Figure 1.4) to visually explain SIT. In addition, Jim shared examples of how he would go through this design thinking process with young learners. For example, the children would suggest a current idea or object and then work through the SIT process to see how they could innovate. Two examples are provided of this process, the first one with a pencil and the second one with a soccer ball (Figures 1.5 and 1.6). For younger learners, the teacher can go through the SIT process with them; older children can work through it alone or with a partner.

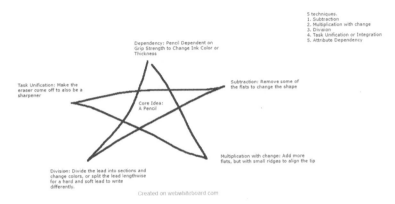

Figure 1.5 Jim provided this example of a pencil and how the steps of SIT can be used to think of ways to make changes to the core idea/object. Photo credit: Jim Butt

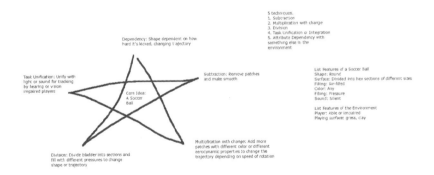

Figure 1.6 In this example using a soccer ball, Jim explained that the ideas generated do not have to "work," but rather, the focus is on thinking through the process. However, innovative ideas often can and do come out of this process. Photo credit: Jim Butt

Tolerance and Inclusivity Training: If situations arise in the classroom that involve intolerance, demonstrate the importance of speaking up to teach tolerance and inclusivity. Teaching Tolerance (tolerance.org) provides many online and free resources for teachers to help them with issues related to diversity, equity, and justice. As Marian Wright Edelman has said, "If we don't stand up for children, then we don't stand for much." Teachers should use these opportunities to teach children about these issues, helping students work together to develop alternative ways to handle difficult situations.

Photography and Video Exploration: Have children take photographs and videos that relate to a particular topic. For example, if you are learning about weather, have students use their digital cameras or iPads to photograph or video the weather and then share with the class. Having pictures and videos to refer back to and explore will serve as visual reinforcers for students to help them remember important concepts they've learned. Additionally, students will learn creative skills related to photography and videography, and rather than just taking pictures and recording video, they can expand into more advanced photo and video editing. Apps such as iPhoto and iMovie provide easy-to-use templates and frameworks to help teachers facilitate this process with young children.

Tips to Practice and Foster Creativity

- Model creative thinking and talk about creativity and innovation in your teaching.
- Encourage risk-taking when learning and create an environment that embraces mistakes.
- Try something new that you haven't tried before.
- Reflect on what worked and didn't work, and then adjust accordingly.

Using Technology Purposefully

Whether or not to use technology with young learners has been a long-standing discussion within the field. In fact, the joint position statement issued by the National Association for the Education of Young Children (NAEYC) and the Fred Rogers Center (FRC) for Early Learning and Children's Media at Saint Vincent College (2012) was established to provide guidance to early-childhood professionals who plan to integrate technology and digital tools while working with young children. We also want to ensure that children learn to be digital citizens and are safe when using technology. According to the Student Standard for digital citizen, students "engage in positive, safe, legal and ethical behavior when using technology, including social interactions online or when using networked devices" (ISTE, 2016). For young learners, as they are just beginning to access technology and learn how to be digital citizens, adults have the responsibility to advocate and verify children are safe when it comes to technology integration.

According to the NAEYC and the Fred Rogers Center, there are several key points to keep in mind when considering the use of technology with young students:

- If tools are used appropriately, young children can learn through technology and digital media.
- If teachers and administrators use technology, they should be aware of resources and information related to the technology or digital media.
- Children need limits set on technology use and digital media.
- Awareness of digital equity and digital citizenship is important to keep in mind.
- Continually learning about and researching the use of technology with young children is critical.

The use of technology is inevitable, and teachers can be purposeful about using it as a tool to encourage innovation and creativity. We live in a technology-saturated society where learners have access to a plethora of information and digital tools that are changing constantly. In addition, learners can collaborate and interact with almost anyone using technology (Partnership for 21st Century Learning [P21], 2016). Because digital tools are changing constantly, it is important to note that what matters most is not the specific technology being used, but the learning that's occurring and whether the technology use is developmentally appropriate. Vaidyanathan (2012) stated that "digital design is neither learning about technology nor learning with technology, but learning creativity and innovation through technology" (p. 25). The purposeful use of technology can aid students with disabilities and also English Language Learners by providing them with tools to scaffold their learning. The Office of Educational Technology (n.d.) provided the following Call to Action brief regarding technology use with early learners:

> When evaluating and recommending technology for use with early learners, consideration should be given to how the child is using the technology, including the quality of the content, the context for its use, and the involvement of adults and peers. With the plethora of new technologies and the active ways they can be used, families and early educators should take a more nuanced approach than simply

thinking about screen time limits and evaluate the content, context, and their child's development to determine what is appropriate in each circumstance. (para. 6)

The subskills listed under the P21 Framework for 21st Century Learning can guide teachers' decisions on whether a specific technology will inspire students to be creative and innovative. Teachers can also ask themselves some questions to help make these decisions: Is the technology helping the child think creatively? Are students working creatively with others? Are they able to implement innovations?

Here are a few ways to integrate technology and build on creativity and innovation within your classroom:

- Encourage children to use technology to take pictures/videos and then make up stories using these pictures or videos. Props can be provided to facilitate creative thinking.
- Use a free videoconferencing tool (for example, Skype, Zoom, Google Hangouts) to collaborate with another school or classroom, and have children ask questions about the other students' communities and lives.
- Coding can be done with scaffolding by teachers or families as early as preschool. Some free websites to teach coding include Scratch (scratch.mit.edu/parents) and Code.org (code.org/learn). The Science Kiddo website (sciencekiddo.com/coding-preschool) provides ways to teach preschoolers and kindergartners the basics of coding without a computer or device.

Empowering Children to Set Personal Goals

When we think about empowering learners and especially young learners, we need to provide them with support and guidance to become self-directed and proactive learners. One way to do this is to teach them how to set personal goals. This is also something that families can support from home. It is never too early to discuss with young children the ability for them to set SMART goals (Specific, Measurable, Attainable, Relevant, and Timely). Having an approach such as SMART can help teachers seamlessly build developing these skills into the curriculum and can guide students as they process their thinking and the goals they aspire to meet.

Connell (2016) has provided multiple suggestions for how to set SMART goals with your students and included templates available for download on her blog on the

Scholastic website (goo.gl/nmYJ2C). Even before children are writing, you can talk to them about setting SMART goals and have them draw pictures of something they want to learn how to do. If young children think about creativity and talk about their ideas early on, they will be more comfortable becoming actively involved in their own learning.

Allowing young learners to be part of the larger discussion surrounding the day's learning outcomes is particularly powerful. Not only does it introduce the content for the day to students, but it also allows students to think about what they will learn and connect it to the activities they will be engaged in. This gives students agency over their own learning and can provide teachers with initial feedback about what students already know about the subject matter.

Addressing Concerns over Using Technology with Young Children

When technology is integrated purposefully and with adult support, it can be a way to increase learning and provide 24-7 learning opportunities. The Student Standards suggest ways to keep children safe and to ensure they learn how to be digital citizens (ISTE, 2016). However, many teachers and families are nervous about certain types of technology use, and we need to listen to and validate these concerns. Helene, for example, encourages creativity in her young students, but is hesitant about integrating technology:

> I try to keep the girls as far away as I can from technology because I feel like they see it now more as a thing to play games on than as a tool. This means, I guess, that I should start to show them that it is a tool, but I feel like their motor skills are still developing, and I would rather have them paint and use scissors to develop that dexterity.
>
> One thing we did do this fall that has nothing to do with technology, but that I think the girls really liked, was we went for a hike through the reservation where there is a fairy garden (Figure 1.7). The girls brought their journals and sketched some of the houses—which was great—but next time, I think I would have them do that and bring their "little-kid" cameras to take pics (Figure 1.8). When we got home, we collected sticks and animal-friendly material in our yard to make our own fairy house. They seemed to get a kick out of it.

As mentioned previously, organizations such as NAEYC have created guidelines and best practices for developmentally appropriate use of technology. Teachers and families can tap into their resources and use them as a framework and guide for safe and appropriate technology integration for young children. Here are some examples of the learning activities suggested by NAEYC (2016) that demonstrate effective classroom practice involving technology tools and interactive media:

- Videotape children while interacting with dramatic play areas and let children watch and comment on their dramatic play experiences.
- Record children's stories using audio or video and use these recordings to document learning as well as discuss learning with families.
- Use videoconferencing tools to communicate with families and children who are in other locations.

Figure 1.7 Taking a hike through fairy gardens encourages children's imagination and creativity. Photo credit: Helene McKelvey McLaughlin

It is important to note that beyond technology use are opportunities, such as what Helene described, for students to be creative. In addition, there are simple ways to tie in technology on a more basic level; for example, to extend young children's learning and sharing, you could have them take a photo of their work and post it on Pinterest. Or, have children record their stories (as in a story about a fairy house) via audio or video to share with families and discuss learning. These activities may inspire other teachers or parents to create similar projects for their children and students, respectively.

Collaboration to Support Creativity and Innovation

Figure 1.8 Allowing children to explore inspires creativity and innovation. Photo credit: Helene McKelvey McLaughlin

Sometimes our most creative ideas come from others. Finding the time to discuss ideas is not always easy during a busy school day, but teachers should look out for ways to collaborate and communicate on ideas to incorporate innovation and creativity in their teaching and to also involve families and communities. In doing so, they can help bring creativity and innovation to their classrooms and beyond, thereby redefining teaching and learning.

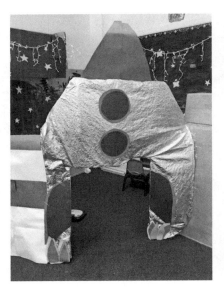

Figure 1.9 Lori turned her classroom into a space center and involved families in the process by collecting materials and contributions for the space design. Photo credit: Lori Griggs

Figure 1.10 The space center theme encouraged children to explore science, and families contributed to the redesign by donating materials. Photo credit: Lori Griggs

Sharing with families the importance of developing creativity and innovation in young children is a good first step in involving them in encouraging these important digital age skills. It may be helpful to explain in a newsletter or bulletin board display how children are thinking creatively, working creatively together, and implementing innovations in the classroom. Technology can also provide a way for families to see what their children are doing in the classroom; for example, photos (as long as permission has been provided by families) can be shared on a school blog or classroom Facebook page. An event can be planned to encourage making and innovation by inviting the families and the community to showcase the work that is being done in the classroom. Families can also have opportunities to create and explore making at the family and community event.

In addition to attending events and viewing artwork, family involvement can also be enhanced by inviting them to participate at the planning process stage. Doing so can demonstrate to families and students that their input is just as valuable as the feedback from teachers and other individuals from the school. Families also become encouraged to take ownership in their contributions and to be more engaged in planning and implementing activities and events.

Figure 1.11 Adding a carnival theme to their learning space provided children with opportunities to practice math skills by integrating a cash register as well as tickets that children could win and count. Photo credit: Lori Griggs

Figure 1.12 The castle theme allowed children to role play and enjoy exploring. Photo credit: Lori Griggs

Figure 1.13 Children had fun in this redesigned classroom as they pretended to live in a castle. Photo credit: Lori Griggs

Redesigning learning spaces is another way for teachers to collaborate with families and students. For example, one teacher, Lori, collaborated with families and redesigned the learning space in her classroom to encourage creativity and innovation (Figures 1.9 and 1.10).

Lori used materials such as aluminum foil, mural paintings of stars, and creative contributions from students and their families. By sharing her ideas outside of her classroom and school, she created a ripple effect of creative thinking and innovation, which gave other teachers ideas of how to redesign learning spaces. A few months later, Lori redesigned the classroom into a carnival theme (Figure 1.11). The carnival theme included a ring toss, a ticket center, and park maps, and it provided activities that integrated content such as math, social studies, science, and the creative arts. Lori continues to find creative ways to redesign learning spaces in her classroom, and her latest redesign captured a castle theme (Figure 1.12 and 1.13).

Loren, who teaches second grade, is another teacher who redesigns learning spaces. She provided photos of her classroom turned into a train station (Figure 1.14). She also provided flexible seating options to her students, so that they could sit in train

Figure 1.14 Loren's second-grade students enjoy learning in their classroom that is redesigned as a train station. Photo credit: Loren Loomis

Figure 1.15 Young children enjoy flexible seating options. In Loren's second-grade classroom, students can sit in a train car while learning. Photo credit: Loren Loomis

cars while learning (Figure 1.15). These inspirational examples provide many ideas for how to create a fun, theme-based learning environment.

Exercise 1.3 can help teachers think through ways they can redefine learning spaces in their classroom to help foster creativity. As mentioned previously, we feel an important part of this process is to involve families in the redesign and ask them to help with the design or to provide materials to include in the learning spaces.

>> Exercise 1.3 Redesigning Learning Spaces Activity

Redesigning Learning Spaces to Nurture Creativity in Young Learners

Theme:

How can you redesign your learning spaces to represent this theme?

What materials do you need?

How can you include families?

How can you extend this activity?

You can access Exercise 1.3 on our wiki and also at tinyurl.com/NYI-redesign.

If Doing This... Why Not Try This? »»»»

Flexible Seating: If using flexible seating within your classroom, including adding materials like yoga mats, bath mats, crates, and large pillows

Redesign Your Classroom Around a Theme: Incorporate the flexible seating into a specific redesign theme (for example, see Figures 1.11 through 1.15) and enlist the skills of family members and the community if applicable.

Here are some suggestions:

- Find out your students' interests and passions and create a theme around these ideas. This is also a good opportunity to engage a child with special needs who may have a specific interest you can focus on.
- Request donations from families for recycled and household materials that can be used to redesign the space.
- Recruit family or community volunteers who may be able to provide special skills needed to redesign the space. Ensure your space is inclusive of all children in your classroom and provide accommodations whenever necessary.

Sand Table: If using the sand table to explore with funnels and measuring cups

Incorporate Tech Tools with Sand Table Exploration: Use the sand table to have children dig for dinosaur bones and provide them with technology tools so they can dig deeper. For example, one kindergarten class in the southeastern United States provided children with a digital camera, online drawing software, and microscopes (U.S. Department of Education, 2016). Adults working with these students taught them how to use the tools and provided them with support, which helped the kindergarteners to observe, discuss, and represent their thinking.

Writing Letters to Military Professionals: If doing a class service project in which children write letters and send care packages to military professionals

Connect Online with Military Professionals: Connect with military professionals using Skype or Google Hangouts and let the children ask questions and communicate. Before the event, have students collaborate and develop the questions they will ask while on the call. Afterward, collect and send care packages to the military professionals.

Take Apart Center: If collecting and taking apart electronics

Create an Upcycled Inventor's Box: Create an upcycled inventor's box. Within the box, have recycled materials (water bottles; plastic lids, caps, and cups; buttons; toilet paper rolls), craft materials (pom-poms, yarn, string, paper, feathers), tools (scissors, glue, tape, hot glue gun—used only by the adults, not the children, for safety reasons). The young learners can make inventions using the many items in the box.

Projects to Nurture Young Innovators

This section provides sample projects to help nurture young innovators. The Common Core State Standards are integrated to help show how these projects are connected to the standards and to illustrate what students should be able to do after taking part in them.

What-if Question Genie for Creative Writing

This project can be used with children ages 5 to 8.

CCSS.ELA-Literacy.W.2.3: *Write narratives in which they recount a well-elaborated event or short sequence of events, include details to describe actions, thoughts, and feelings, use temporal words to signal event order, and provide a sense of closure.*

Bruce Van Patter created the What if? Genie to encourage creative writing. When students click on the What if? Genie, a question is generated. The students can then begin their creative writing from the prompt they receive. Give it a try on his website (www.brucevanpatter.com/what_if_questions.php).

This activity can be modified for younger children or English Language Learners by having them draw instead of write to demonstrate the prompt generated by the Genie. According to the Common Core State Standards Initiative (2017), young children need opportunities to "use a combination of drawing, dictating, and writing to compose informative/explanatory texts in which they name what they are writing about and supply some information about the topic" (CCSS.ELA-Literacy.W.K2). This will help children develop these important skills while thinking creatively.

Make Your Own Fairy or Dinosaur Garden

The standards addressed are for Grade 1, but this activity can be done for a range of grades (PK to Grade 2).

CCSS.ELA-Literacy.SL.1.4: *Describe people, places, things, and events with relevant details, expressing ideas and feelings clearly.*

This activity can be done in school or also extended and completed at home. One way to involve the family is to have each child create their own home for their dinosaur or fairy at home and bring it in to the class garden. When children participate in creating their own fairy or dinosaur gardens, they will also demonstrate speaking and listening and being able to present their knowledge and ideas on the people, places, and events in their gardens.

Here are suggestions for the project:

- Materials: Children can go on a scavenger hunt to find materials outside for their gardens; for example, flower pots, Popsicle sticks, buttons, glue, feathers, plastic dinosaurs, plastic fairies, or plants (the ideas are endless, but the more creative the better).
- Technology integration: Children can take a video of their fairy or dinosaur gardens and describe the people, places, and things within them.
- Refer to the "Fairy Gardens" Pinterest board (https://www.pinterest.com/ltaddei2/fairy-gardens) for ideas on how to create fairy gardens.
- Watch *The Gnomist* (2014), a documentary by Sharon Liese that tells the story of a real-life fairy garden in Overland Park, Kansas. Read more about the film at its website (thegnomistfilm.com).

Exercise 1.4 is an action plan for nurturing young innovators and cultivating creativity. We believe teachers benefit from creating action plans and setting SMART goals when it comes to intentionally creating an atmosphere where innovation and creativity exist.

✛ Reflection Questions

Here are some questions to consider after you've completed this chapter:

- How do you foster creativity with the young learners you are working with?
- Empowered learners are given choices and encouraged to think creatively. How do you help children know they are empowered learners and that you encourage them to think creatively?
- How do you assess creativity and innovation when working with young learners?
- How can you use Systematic Inventive Thinking within your classroom? How can this kind of thinking/process benefit early learners?
- How do you involve families in creative ways?
- How do you decide which tools, apps, and technology to use within your classroom?
- In what ways do you help children learn about being a responsible, safe digital citizen?
- After reading this chapter, what is one thing you will try that you have not done before?

›› Exercise 1.4 Action Plan for Nurturing Young Innovators and Cultivating Creativity

Describe your ideas and methods for nurturing young innovators and cultivating creativity in the classroom, home, and community.

Actions steps you will take to accomplish this goal (include what, why, when, and how):

What challenges do you foresee?

What supports/resources do you need to accomplish your goals?

Reflection:

Additional notes and comments:

You can access a downloadable version of this action plan (Exercise 1.4) on our wiki (nurturingyounginnovators.wikispaces.com/Resources).

Building a Community for Risk-Taking and Innovation

"Vulnerability is the birthplace of innovation, creativity and change."

—*Brené Brown*

I f we expect our students to take risks and try new things, we as educators need to model the idea of risk-taking responsibly. This chapter provides practical ways to do so within schools and classrooms and shows how to encourage this mindset within families and communities.

According to the ISTE Standards for Educators, teachers should "continually improve their practice by learning from and with others and exploring proven and promising practices that leverage technology to improve student learning" (International Society for Technology in Education [ISTE], 2017). For teachers to be global collaborators and leaders in using digital tools and resources, they need continual opportunities to engage in professional growth and learning. With this in mind, in this chapter we'll share tools and ideas for creating professional and personal learning networks to help support an environment of risk-taking, innovation, and community building.

Chapter Overview

This chapter will cover the following:

- Supporting students as innovative designers
- Encouraging risk-taking in teachers so they can model responsible risk-taking for students

- Creating a trauma-sensitive environment that supports healthy risk-taking
- Techniques for supporting risk-taking in the classroom and beyond
- Reflection questions specific to experimenting with new technologies and teaching methods

Student as Innovative Designer

"Students use a variety of technologies within a design process to identify and solve problems by creating new, useful or imaginative solutions."

—ISTE Standards for Students, Standard 4: Innovator Designer

According to the Student Standards, "students select and use digital tools to plan and manage a design process that considers design constraints and calculated risks" (ISTE, 2016). Also stated within this standard is that students should "exhibit a tolerance for ambiguity, perseverance and the capacity to work with open-ended problems" (ISTE, 2016).

For students to be able to take risks, they need to be able to work through problems and uncertainty, skills which require creativity and innovative thinking. Technology can be used in a variety of ways to foster creativity while encouraging children to consider and manage risk. For example, many classrooms and schools are using tablets to enhance student learning. With the use of a tablet, young children can

> brainstorm ideas together, develop various alternatives to solve problems, share ideas and work, and develop solutions using various technology tools, such as 3D printers, painting tools, cloud-based notebooks, composition tools, and interactive management solutions for tablets and electronic boards. (Kim, Park, Yoo, & Kim, 2015, p. 207)

When tablets are used interactively in the classroom, they can help young children develop creativity by learning to express their ideas in a variety of ways (Kim et al., 2015). But the open-endedness of the tablet provides many options to choose from, and trying out a new tool can be risky for some teachers and students. Although making decisions and trying new things can bring about uncertainty, taking risks can also actually promote the development of skills such as perseverance and problem solving. Encouraging teachers and students to take a chance can enable them to take calculated risks.

When choosing activities involving tablets, be sure to include opportunities for students to collaborate and share creative ideas with one another. Giving students opportunities to choose which tool they will use also encourages risk-taking.

This is just one way to look at how to introduce and encourage risk-taking for young children. But where and how can children learn these skills?

Teachers as Risk Takers

Risk-taking looks different for different people. For one student, a risk may be raising his or her hand or trying a new activity. For another, it could mean building a robot from found materials, similar to the preservice teachers in Figure 2.1. But before we even think about risk-taking in terms of young children, we need to have safe environments where teachers, students, and administrators feel it's acceptable to make mistakes. Teachers—supported by administrators, peers, and families—must be able to embrace risk-taking as productive and integral to their classroom environment in order for students to be encouraged as risk takers.

Figure 2.1 Preservice teachers engage in risk-taking behavior by building robots from household materials for the first time.

A blog post from Schools That Work captured risk-taking in a way that shows how important teachers are in supporting risk-taking: "So risk is what we allow and expect in our classrooms—risk combined with abundant opportunity and the safety of being treated as a cherished individual" (Thornton, 2015, p. 1). Indeed, when things do not work as planned, it creates an opportunity to talk about how to learn from mistakes, reflecting on what can be done differently, and trying again. Thornton (2015) described the need for risk-taking and how it works best when supported at all levels:

> Teachers learn to learn from each other as well when spaces for risk become the norm, and the same is true for administrators. Creating space for risk begins at the top of any school system. Principals must have space for risk, so that teachers have space for risk, so that students have space for risk. (para. 11)

In our many years working with teachers, we have heard repeatedly how teachers feel they benefit more from having time to talk with one another and share ideas than from any other form of professional development. One district encouraged teachers to collaborate with one another through inquiry and then develop learning plans (McCrea, 2015). The collaborative process, encouraged by the district, helped the teachers take a risk, learn something new, and share their learning with others. When teachers feel comfortable with each other, they can create a safe space that can translate into safe spaces for students within their own classroom settings.

Diane felt that she did not know as much about technology as some of her colleagues did, so integrating technology was not easy for her:

> I fall short in using technology as I am not as tech savvy as the newer and younger teachers. I wish that I could have grown up in the technology era that the younger teachers have been in, as I see how engaging the technology can be with just what I use.

Over time, she observed her colleagues and got ideas from them, and began to take risks in her own classroom. For example, Diane obtained a grant to purchase Kindles for her learning support classroom and described experimenting with this technology:

> The reading program we use in our district utilizes learning videos that are used interactively with the class. In addition, the math program the other teachers use also have parts that can be used interactively. I have Kindles that I use as a reward for my learning support students who come to my room and complete their assignments to the best of their ability.

Diane provided the following advice to other teachers: "I would say learn as much as you can about technology and keep up to date on the newest technology that is available." It's important to stress that what might not be a risk for one person may be a big risk for another. We also recommend trying one new thing at a time and not trying to do too many things at once. As part of the support process around risk-taking, when other teachers or students share that they tried something new, it's important to encourage them and celebrate the risks they are taking.

Co-teaching and collaborating with other teachers can help support teachers like Diane who may not be as comfortable integrating new technologies. Thornton (2015) reiterated:

> People shy away from risks because they fear failure—but what's so bad about failing? Some of the greatest moments of understanding happen after we've "failed." Viewing failure as a typical aspect of the learning process allows a learner to appreciate the need for risks. (para. 6)

Here are some suggestions on simple ways to create space for risk:

- Model risk-taking by trying out something new and letting your students, colleagues, and others know you are trying something for the first time.
- If things don't work out, use this as an opportunity to discuss what happened, what could be done differently, and what was learned from the experience.
- Allow time for informal conversations and community building and time to get to know each other.
- Create a fun environment; for example, integrate activities that are hands-on, engaging, and fun.

Supporting Teachers in Taking Risks

Because many teachers learn from one another and thrive when supported by colleagues who encourage risk-taking, it's important that they continue to build and rely on their personal and professional networks. As suggested earlier, because teachers are the drivers behind risk-taking in their classroom, they need support in creating a classroom environment that ensures that they are willing to take risks so that their students can do the same, improving their learning and development. Within the Educator Standards, the following suggestions are provided to educators on being empowered professionals:

- Set professional learning goals to explore and apply pedagogical approaches made possible by technology and reflect on their effectiveness.
- Pursue professional interests by creating and actively participating in local and global learning networks.

- Stay current with research that supports improved student learning outcomes, including findings from the learning sciences. (ISTE, 2017)

Connecting with other educators and creating a personal and professional learning network "begins and ends with a genuine and sincere effort to connect in order to serve a cause greater than ourselves" (Whitaker, Zoul, & Casas, 2015, p. 2) (Figure 2.2). We have included the stories of teachers, community members, family members, friends, and our undergraduate and graduate students in this book. We collected responses—from across the country (California, Illinois, New Jersey, Pennsylvania, Rhode Island, Wisconsin)—in a Google form that we shared with our social networks, our students, and community members. As teachers, the more we open ourselves up and connect with others to discuss what we are doing with young learners, the more we—and thus, our students—benefit. Because we have access to technology and can connect virtually with anyone we meet, there are no limits to our personal and professional learning networks. As we connect more with others, we can learn from and support one another in taking risks. Creativity and risk-taking in our peers' classrooms can inspire us to also take risks. For example, in Chapter 1, we included images of how teachers redesigned their classrooms. We hope these pictures and stories we collected through our personal and professional network help others redesign their own classrooms to inspire creativity and innovation.

Figure 2.2 These educators are connecting, collaborating, and experimenting with coding at a family and community event. One of the educators in the group had experience with coding and supported the others as they learned and explored something new.

Alyssa appreciates learning from others and felt that professional learning communities provided her with the support to take risks and try out new things in her classroom:

> It's important to make learning fun. Technology is changing and teachers need to stay ahead of the curve. Teachers learn from teachers—I follow several teacher blogs to learn the new and changing apps and websites. I also learned a lot during my Master's program at Neumann University. Professional learning communities (PLCs) are great ways to share ideas with others as well. Since risk-taking can be a new experience in the classroom for me, participating in a professional learning community is a way to gain insights and motivation to try something new.

Twitter is an excellent resource for building a personal and professional learning network and for connecting with others who can share their own ideas and experiences. A few of the stories collected for this book came from requests sent out through Twitter and we connected with others we hadn't met before. For example, I (Laura) saw a Tweet about the Cardboard Challenge (described in Chapter 5) and integrating this within a math classroom. The next day, I implemented the Cardboard Challenge in my teacher education classroom. Some of my students, who are already teaching in classrooms, went on to implement the Cardboard Challenge in their own classrooms. This is a ripple effect of nurturing young innovators—and it all began with one Tweet.

Whitaker, Zoul, and Casas (2015) considered connected educators as those who grow their knowledge base while giving and sharing their own knowledge, and Twitter provides a way to do this globally. If you are already using Twitter, then we recommend that you keep building your professional learning network, looking for those ideas you can implement within your classroom to nurture young learners and sharing ideas others can use to keep the ripple effect going.

If you are not yet on Twitter, here are some first steps:

- Create a free Twitter account.
- Make your user name similar to your actual name so people can find you.
- Add a picture to your profile.
- Search for accounts to follow that you are interested in. Throughout this book, we suggest accounts to follow that correspond with each chapter.
- Start Tweeting or Retweeting things you find that are helpful.
- If you are looking for a certain topic, you can search by the hashtags. For topics related to this chapter, you can search for #edtech.
- Get used to creating messages consisting of 140 characters or less— these will help you get to the point.

Creating Trauma-Sensitive Environments that Support Healthy Risks

Many young children experience adverse childhood experiences (ACEs) and we need to ensure we are creating trauma-sensitive environments in which they can learn. If we want children to feel free to try things out in our classroom and take healthy risks, we need to ensure they feel safe and secure. Statman-Weil (2015) shared the following:

> A significant number of children experience trauma, and the effects can be profound. It is imperative, therefore, that early childhood settings be safe, trauma-sensitive spaces where teachers support children in creating positive self-identities. (p. 73)

When people experience adverse circumstances, it's natural to enter into survival mode in which learning is not the focus or even possible (Souers & Hall, 2016). Sometimes children react to such situations with behavior that is challenging or inappropriate. Maslow's hierarchy of needs is a theory that supports the idea that children cannot learn if their basic needs are unmet and they do not feel safe. Adverse childhood experiences (ACEs), which can include anything that causes undue stress and trauma to children, are becoming more evident and prevalent within early childhood settings (ACE Response, 2017). Some examples include abuse, neglect, violence, mental illness, divorce, death, or an incarcerated family member. ACE Response (2017) reported, "teachers, school administrators, parents, and others within and beyond the education sector are teaming up to create healthy and supportive school environments that promote the academic success of all students" (para. 3). The first step to supporting children with ACEs is to be aware of trauma or the possibility of trauma and create a trauma-sensitive classroom.

Here are some suggestions to help create a trauma-sensitive environment:

- Allow opportunities for students to express their feelings.
- "Look beyond choice and focus on motive" (Souers & Hall, 2016, p. 32).
- Recognize sometimes the behavior is a consequence of what is going on.
- Communicate with other colleagues and share ideas with one another.
- Include families as much as possible and be open and inclusive (Statman-Weil, 2015).
- Model resiliency and embed learning opportunities on how to be more resilient.
- Provide students with opportunities to make better choices through critical and creative thinking.

Community Connections

Creating a Trauma-Sensitive Classroom Environment

Bernadette S. Taddei, M.Ed.

One of my experiences included working in an after-school partial hospital program at a residential home for abused and neglected children. The children attended several public elementary schools during the day. In my experience, school was a safe place where they were the same as everyone else and they could, if only briefly, forget about family tragedies, illness, abuse, addiction, neglect, and other circumstances that temporarily or permanently separated them from one or both of their parents.

The children often faced academic challenges and the public schools worked diligently to provide the assistance each child required to reach their potential. It would be reasonable to assume that exam days or days projects were due would be the most challenging to a child who lived in a residential program (or any situation without both or one parent involved in a child's life) but the days that often brought the most anxiety and pain were the days that some may take for granted: Mother's Day, Father's Day, Valentine's Day, and other holidays, as well as the days surrounding the holiday.

Teachers would often have well-intentioned projects for the students to create—projects full of hearts, flowers, and gifts with "Mom" or "Dad" clearly emblazoned on them, or maybe an essay assignment based on the role of a mother or father, or written assignments about family activities the child participated in during the summer, fall, or winter break.

To reduce trauma, teachers' approaches to these projects and assignments only require that they view them from the child's perspective. For example, if working on a project about mothers, focus on the qualities of a mother that you want to celebrate and acknowledge the roles that other people fill in the lives of many children. So, if the assignment starts off with discussing mothers, approach the word "mother" as a verb. Ask students: What does it mean to "mother" someone? Who are some people in your life who are like a mother or father to you? Do you have people in your lives that take on that role when a mother or father cannot? Do moms and dads need help sometimes? Who might help them? The specific reasons why a mother or father is not present or why they require help don't need to be discussed. It's important to expand the discussion so that all students can fully participate and not feel

(continued on next page)

(continued from previous page)

excluded. Students should feel encouraged to make a gift or write an essay with the flexibility to adapt it to their viewpoint without feeling singled-out.

Teachers need to be prepared that even when these holidays and projects are approached with the utmost compassion, understanding, and openness, a child dealing with trauma may still have a formidable task coping. Mindful of this, students may need space and time to grieve or someone to talk to. Every child, like adults, will manifest this in different ways—physical pain, anger, isolation, or illness.

Small adaptations can go a long way in decreasing or eliminating the pain a child feels when having or experiencing trauma. It's important to be mindful of each child's unique situation and review lessons from his or her perspective and be flexible to allow children to incorporate their unique life situations to each project without fear.

Community Building to Support Risk-Taking

When classrooms and schools focus on community building, this fosters a nurturing and encouraging atmosphere for young children, and ultimately, fosters risk-taking. When people feel connected and safe within their classroom, home, or community, they may be more willing to take chances with learning and to make mistakes. The more we can include families and communities in what we're doing in our classrooms, the more we can build a transparent and open atmosphere where we can share what our students are doing and learning, and the more passionate and excited we all become about learning.

Technology can provide an excellent way to build community in the classroom. For example, Peg shared various ways she and her students use technology to learn and build community:

> We use digital resources such as Office 365, SharePoint, and Skype to interact with my students. We share documents, interact in discussion boards, and Skype during and after school hours. Letting students communicate digitally with me and their peers creates enthusiasm for learning during and after school hours. Students who do not share much in school have shared more online with the class. I get to see another side of my students, and they can't wait to learn new ways to communicate and find new friends and family to communicate with. I also have

videos of me in our OneNote for Classroom that students can use for new learning or a reteach of something they've already been introduced to.

The most effective way to engage families, and thus build community, is to ensure the technology provides for two-way communication (Mitchell, Foulger, & Wetzel, 2009). Sharing photos with families using technology can help build community. Photos can be shared on a class website or on Facebook. We have used multiple free resources to create classroom websites. For example, Wikispaces (wikispaces.com) is free to educators and provides a user-friendly way to create a class website. You can invite families to join the website and also open it up so they can contribute to the website if appropriate. Google Sites is also an easy-to-use option. Whatever option works for you is the one you should use.

Pinterest provides an easy way to collaborate and share ideas. Families can follow teacher or school Pinterest boards, and they can share their own boards too. As we were writing this book, we also used Pinterest to share ideas that were relevant to topics within our chapters. Here are links to our Pinterest pages related to topics in this book.

Pinterest Boards Related to Nurturing Young Innovators

- Nurturing Young Innovators (www.pinterest.com/ltaddei2/nurturing younginnovators)
- Family Involvement Ideas (www.pinterest.com/ltaddei2/family-involvement -ideas)
- Trauma-Sensitive Classroom (www.pinterest.com/ltaddei2/trauma -sensitive-classroom)
- Random Acts of Kindness (www.pinterest.com/ltaddei2/random-act -of-kindness-ideas)
- Makerspace Ideas (www.pinterest.com/ltaddei2/makerspace-ideas)
- Creative Arts, PK to fourth grade (www.pinterest.com/ltaddei2/ creative-arts-ece-245)
- Science Methods, PK to fourth grade (www.pinterest.com/ltaddei2/ science-methods-ece-315)
- Math Methods, PK to fourth grade (www.pinterest.com/ltaddei2/math -methods)

Next, we'll share a few examples of wikis created by our preservice teachers to share ideas and resources. When we first integrated wikis within our classes, there was definitely a risk because this technology tool was new to the students and many were anxious about learning how to use the wiki. We received pushback from students who were fearful of trying something new. With persistence, the wiki creation became a large part of many of our classes. Students became innovative designers and persisted through the ambiguity and found ways to use wikis to share information, collaborate with their peers, and learn new ideas and ways to teach. The preservice teachers created their own lesson plans and found resources to reinforce concepts they were teaching and learning. Here are a few examples:

Math Methods—PK to Grade 1

As part of their class, students in ECE 224 (examples below of Fall 2014 and Spring 2015) created a class wiki that provided resources and suggestions on ways to implement mathematics into PK through first-grade classrooms. Students created and shared lesson plans related to math with their classmates and the broader community:

- ECE 224, Fall 2014 (mathmethodsfall2014nu.wikispaces.com)
- ECE 224, Spring 2015 (mathmethods1spring2015.wikispaces.com)

Science Methods—PK to Grade 4

As part of their class, students in ECE 315, Science Methods—PK to Grade 4, created a class wiki. This wiki assignment provided resources and suggestions on ways to implement science into PK through fourth-grade classrooms. Students in this course added resources that provided support and suggestions for teaching science to young children.

- ECE 315, Fall 2014 (sciencemethodsnu.wikispaces.com)
- ECE 315, Spring 2015 (sciencemethodsspring2015.wikispaces.com)

Integrating the Arts—PK to Grade 4

As part of their class, students in ECE 245, Integrating the Arts—PK to Grade 4, created a class wiki. This wiki assignment provided resources and suggestions on ways to integrate the arts into PK through fourth-grade classrooms. Students in this course added resources on the pages of this wiki that provided support and suggestions for integrating the arts.

- ECE 245, Fall 2014 (integratedartsnu.wikispaces.com)
- ECE 245, Spring 2015 (integratedartsspring2015.wikispaces.com)

Techniques for Supporting Risk-Taking in the Classroom and Beyond

Young learners need opportunities to take risks, and in this section we provide suggestions on how to support them in the classroom, home, and community. First, we'll discuss the importance of play in helping children take risks. Next, we'll address focusing on the process rather than the product so that learners can create and innovate without worrying about making mistakes. Finally, we share ways to teach above the line and use technology tools to modify and redefine learning.

Encouraging Risk-Taking Through Play

Play is an excellent vehicle to help encourage risk-taking in young children. Young children thrive when they play, and play brings people together and helps to relieve stress. Free play for young children is "a great way for them to focus on creative thinking, which allows them to forget what is troubling them." (Voice of Play, n.d.) Kevin Carroll (2012) described play as a way to change a life in his TEDxHarlem video (https://youtu.be/1pz72Wygg8c). Within this video, Carroll (2012) stated, "Play is serious business. Play is at the root of creativity, problem solving, abstract thinking, imagination, innovation." Carroll provides additional ideas about play and how sports and play can change the world on his website (kevincarrollkatalyst.com). Children are natural adventurers and curious. They need planned opportunities to explore. Almon (2013) reiterated, "when children are given a chance to engage freely in adventurous play they quickly learn to assess their own skills and match them to the demands of the environment." Through adventurous play, children are allowed to take chances and they become more confident and resilient, which are both characteristics of risk-taking.

In Chapter 1, we shared multiple ideas on how teachers have redesigned learning spaces to support imaginative thinking and risk-taking. For example, when inside their classroom redesigned as a train station (Figure 1.14) and seated in their train car (Figure 1.15), children can imagine they are going on an adventure to anywhere. In this example, technology could also be integrated by having children use Google Earth to look at different locations they will be visiting on their train ride. Videoconferencing tools can be used to connect with classrooms in different schools. The use of these tools can redefine learning because children can use their imagination to take the trips and then talk with children who live in these areas, making connections to real life.

In addition, play experiences embedded within classrooms and connected to curriculum can expose children to areas they may have otherwise never been interested in. For example, the space center–themed classroom included in Chapter 1 (Figure 1.10) could spark science-related adventures and interests for young learners. To integrate technology in this design, one example would be to include virtual tours that help children have a more visual experience with the topic. For the space center theme, students can experience a virtual tour of the International Space Center at Space.com (tinyurl.com/NYI-spacetour). In addition, NASA provides many free resources for educators organized by grade level (tinyurl.com/NYI-nasa). This is also a great way to engage both boys and girls in STEAM (science, technology, engineering, the arts, math) topics (discussed more in the next section and in Chapter 5).

As suggested in the NSTA (National Science Teachers Association) (2009) position statement on Parent Involvement in Science Learning:

> Seek out opportunities to introduce your children to individuals in your community whose work relates to science or technology. This may include trades and professions such as construction or manufacturing, public safety, medicine, natural resource management, or research. (para. 7)

In Chapter 1, community member Jim Butt shared how he visited his school district in partnership with his local company and talked to students about innovation and his work as an aerospace engineer. Similar to classroom redesign themes, these types of visits and experiences can spark interest in students that may encourage them to try something new or lead to a lifelong interest and a career they love and are passionate about.

Process over Product

In order for children to feel that it's safe to take risks, they have to know mistakes are accepted and not penalized. Reynolds (n.d.) stated, "without risk, there is no challenge, and consequently, there is no growth. Both physical and intellectual risks are vital to the normal development of a child." Oftentimes, children are concerned about grades; and therefore, they may be hesitant to take risks if they're worried that doing so will affect their grades. Connecting the grade to the process instead of the final product would help create an atmosphere where risk is supported and even rewarded. Defors (2016) shared a rubric (tinyurl.com/NYI-risktakingrubric) created to grade the process not the product. Although this rubric was developed for older students, it could be modified to work for younger learners too.

STEAM projects often provide children with an opportunity to focus on the process and not the final product. Because STEAM projects can be very open-ended, children may worry about whether they are doing something right or not. Assuring children that the process is more important than the final product will help alleviate their concerns. In Chapter 5, we share specific STEAM ideas and ways to engage children in these activities that encourage risk-taking while nurturing innovative designers.

Teaching above the Line

When we think of risk-taking related to technology integration, we think of teaching above the line as described by Puentedura (2009) with the use of the SAMR (Substitution, Augmentation, Modification, Redefinition) model. Many times, when technology is integrated, it may be used as either a Substitution or an Augmentation to learning. Teaching above the line takes learning beyond Substitution and Augmentation, and learning is Modified or Redefined with the use of technology. We believe technology integration needs to be thought through and intentional, and reflecting after the activity or lesson is also an excellent way to evaluate the learning. We use the SAMR model developed by Puentedura (2009) when planning and deciding on technology integration. Without support and ideas, technology may mainly be used as a Substitution (acts as a substitute, but with no real change) or Augmentation (acts as a substitute with improvement in function). Schrock (2013) provides a multitude of suggestions on ways to teach above the line and move toward Modification (technology allows for significant task design) and Redefinition (technology redefines the learning and allows for something that would be impossible without the use of technology). Schrock (2013) provides further examples, videos, and charts to explain the SAMR model in more detail on her website Kathy Schrock's Guide to Everything (schrockguide.net/samr.html). We stress that the focus is not on the tool, but the learning.

We have developed a list of activities that include technologies used to encourage creativity and innovation in young children, differentiated for various grade levels, and defining where the idea falls along the SAMR ladder and why (ie., Substitution, Augmentation, Modification, and Redefinition [Table 2.1]). You can download a blank template on our wiki (nurturingyounginnovators.wikispaces.com/Resources) and modify it for your own reflection on teaching above the line and using the SAMR model.

Table 2.1 Creativity/Innovation Technology Activities Using SAMR Model

Activity	Grade Level	Technology Used	SAMR Level
Creative Arts: Students explore Van Gogh's art and then draw their own version of one of Van Gogh's pieces.	Grade 3	Instead of using paper and drawing material, students can create their artwork on their mobile device. They could use Sketchpad or Doodle Pad.	Substitution: technology acts as a substitution and there is no functional change.
English Language Arts: Students brainstorm and create a digital poster or mind map of a topic they've researched.	Grade 3	Popplet (mind map tool), MindMeister (brainstorming tool)	Augmentation: technology acts as a tool substitution and there's some functional improvement.
Math: Introduce children to computer programming and coding. Early learners start with symbols.	K to Grade 2	Kodable, Code.org, or ScratchJr—make sure whatever technology you choose allows children to build and create.	Modification: With the addition of the technology, the task is redesigned.
Science: Find simple machines in action, take photos of them, then use stop motion software and/or create a commercial.	Grade 2	Students can choose what technology to use, but some suggestions include recording with a digital camera, iPad, or mobile device, or using a stop motion software tool. Examples are PaintShop Pro animation studio, Stop Motion Studio, and MonkeyJam.	Modification: with the addition of the technology, the task is redesigned.
Social Studies: Connect with a classroom in another community and have students conduct interviews and ask one another questions.	PK to Grade 2	Skype, Google Hangouts	Redefinition: this activity couldn't occur without the use of technology, demonstrating a redefinition of learning.

If Doing This... Why Not Try This?

If Doing This...	Why Not Try This?
Twitter for Professional Development. If using Twitter to follow applicable feeds as a professional development tool	**Use Twitter Chat.** If already using Twitter, why not take part in a Twitter Chat? We found a great Twitter chat on risk-taking that goes well with this chapter. Check out Mark Barnes' Hack Learning website (hacklearning.org) and find the next #HackLearning Twitter chat. You can also find archives for past #HackLearning chats, such as this Twitter chat on Improving Ed Tech in Schools (goo.gl/bjE2mR).
Experimenting with New Technology. If trying out a new technology tool in your classroom	**Collaborate with Colleagues.** Partner with colleagues and decide to collaborate with the use of technology on specific course content. For example, create a wiki and collaborate as a means to share professional development resources.
Using YouTube Videos. If using videos in your classroom to support learning	**Teacher YouTube Channel.** Create your own YouTube channel and record videos of class activities and share with families and the community. Also have your students create their own videos and share them on the YouTube channel.
Following Blogs as Professional Development. If you follow blogs to learn about educational technology	**Start Blogging and Sharing What You Know.** A good place to start is Edublogs, a free and easy-to-use resource for educators (edublogs.org).

Projects for Building Community to Support Risk-Taking

We recommend engaging families and communities and inviting them to events where they can come and engage and have fun. Such events can build community, promote risk-taking through play, and demonstrate the benefits of collaboration. This connects with the Educator Standards, as teachers are called to "demonstrate cultural competency when communicating with students, parents and colleagues and interact with them as co-collaborators in student learning" (ISTE, 2017).

Global School Day of Play

This project can be used for any grade level.

The Global School Play Day provides a way to advocate for play in schools, classrooms, and community. There's a Global School Play Day every year, but schools can either join in and participate on the global day or create their own day of play. Given that many schools are eliminating or reducing play in the classroom, this is a wonderful initiative to raise awareness of the importance of unstructured play.

Note that children can bring in toys to play with for the day of play, but the tools should not have batteries. Also during the day of play, there should be no screens and children should choose how to play and what to play. Play is student-driven and unstructured.

Here's how to get started:

- You can sign up using Google Forms on the Global School Play Day website (globalschoolplayday.com).
- Advertise your school's Global School Play Day by sharing information about the event with families, colleagues, students, and community members to engage everyone. Peter Gray's TEDx video "The Decline of Play" (https://youtu.be/Bg-GEzM7iTk) can be used to demonstrate what it's all about.

Family Night: QR Code Scavenger Hunt

This project can be used for any grade level.

Figure 2.3 Here is an example of a QR code we created that links to our family survey. If someone does not want to use the QR code, they could also use the link (kaywa. me/9Pm6b) to get there.

Create a scavenger hunt, and use a QR generator to create QR codes of a Google form you created (Figure 2.3). Families can scan the QR code with a free QR code reader and then submit answers into the form. Each QR code they find will be different, and they will scan each one and submit their responses, watch a video, find out where to go next, and so on.

Here are the steps to do this:

1. Create a QR code to link to websites or resources you want families to explore. We provide suggested ideas on areas you can link to for this family scavenger hunt; however, we encourage you to come up with your own ideas. You decide how many QR codes to use and where the QR codes will link to provide further information to families. For instance, the following QR codes could be posted around the classroom for families to scan with a QR reader (or, if they aren't comfortable using a QR reader, they can use the URLs provided):

    - **A short family survey using Google Forms** (tinyurl.com/ NYI-familyscavengerhunt) prompting the families to explore different areas of the school and classroom. They can answer the questions on the form online as they walk along and also scan different QR codes placed around the room.

    - **A class wiki or school website;** example of a wiki created by one of the authors (tinyurl.com/NYI-drtaddeiwiki)

    - **A presentation to let families know about their student's teacher;** example of a Prezi (tinyurl.com/NYI-drtaddeiprezi) one of the authors used to introduce herself to students (although this example is at the college level, it can be used at any level)

    - **A Padlet page** (https://padlet.com/ltaddei/ew777rs9po0z); you can ask families to add pictures of their family/child to the page

2. Copy the link for each resource into a free QR generator. We used Kaywa.com (qrcode.kaywa.com).
3. Print the QR codes and post around the school/classroom.

Note that families will need to download free QR readers on their phones/mobile devices. There are many to choose from. You can also have mobile devices available and ready with QR readers for families to use to complete the scavenger hunt.

Kathy Schrock's Guide to Everything (schrockguide.net/qr-codes-in-the-classroom. html) offers many other ideas for how to integrate QR codes in the classroom.

Here's a good example of a QR code tree that families can scan to find out information about Murray Hill Middle School in Howard County, Maryland (www.flickr.com/photos/info_grrl/6158600469). This QR activity can be created for any school.

+ Reflection Questions

Here are some questions to consider after you've completed this chapter:

- What kind of risks do you plan to take in your classroom or school? How will you encourage children to take risks?
- What are some ways you help to create an environment where mistakes are embraced and where we learn from our mistakes?
- How can you create a trauma-sensitive classroom?
- What are the challenges you may face when encouraging risk-taking?
- How can you support your peers when it comes to embracing technology and trying something new?
- How can you embed more time for children to play and explore to encourage risk-taking and innovative? Children are naturally adventurous. How can you create environments that encourage adventure?
- How can you encourage children to be innovative designers and to persevere when taking part in open-ended and ambiguous activities?
- After reading this chapter, what is one thing you will try that you have not done before?

Collaborating with Families on Student Learning

"Coming together is a beginning, staying together is progress, and working together is success."

— Henry Ford

Collaborating with families to support their children's learning is extremely important, and teachers should make it a priority in their classrooms. In fact, Garcia and Thornton (2014) noted that "the most significant type of involvement is what parents do at home. By monitoring, supporting and advocating, parents can be engaged in ways that ensure that their children have every opportunity for success" (p.1). There must be mechanisms in place to facilitate assisting parents in supporting their children at home. Because technology is such a dynamic and flexible tool, there are many ways to leverage it to serve as a catalyst to create collaboration between learners and families.

A focus on the redefinition of learning rather than the technology tool itself is important, and you should make sure that when you use technology with families, the focus is on improving communication and collaboration. According to the ISTE Standards for Educators, teachers should "demonstrate cultural competency when communicating with students, parents and colleagues and interact with them as co-collaborators in student learning" (International Society for Technology in Education [ISTE], 2017). Technology can assist us all in helping support young innovators not only in the classroom, but also in the home and the community. In this chapter, we provide multiple ideas on how to involve families as co-collaborators using Epstein's Six Types of Involvement Framework. We address the ISTE Standards for students as well.

Chapter Overview

This chapter will cover the following:

- Students as knowledge constructors
- Connecting families to in-class learning experiences
- Supporting families in fostering innovation in young children
- Consideration for accessibility of technology for families
- Reflection questions specific to supporting families as they encourage innovation in young children

Student as Knowledge Constructor

"Students critically curate a variety of resources using digital tools to construct knowledge, produce creative artifacts and make meaningful learning experiences for themselves and others."

— *ISTE Standards for Students, Standard 3: Knowledge Constructor*

Knowledge construction is an ongoing and iterative process that requires a constant and consistently active learning environment filled with experiential exploration opportunities. As this standard suggests, it is important to provide students the opportunity to locate information and resources that will aid them in understanding their educative experiences. Families and teachers can work together to assist students in building their capacity to leverage a variety of technology and media tools to conceptualize and bring learning to actualization. Students, even young children, must learn how to be critical consumers of information and how to "evaluate the accuracy, perspective, credibility and relevance of information, media, data or other resources" (ISTE, 2016).

Students should be able to "curate information from digital sources using a variety of tools and methods to create collections of artifacts that demonstrate meaningful connections or conclusions" (ISTE, 2016). Because these types of experiences happen inside and outside of the classroom—in the school, classroom library, at home, or the local public library—families must be provided with ways to help students connect what they're learning in school to what is happening in their lives.

Connecting Families to In-Class Learning Experiences

Learning does not happen in isolation, and it certainly transcends the classroom walls. Students can learn in their homes, in the local community, and beyond. Any event, experience, and environment has the potential to lead to teachable moments and learning. It is critical to connect families to their children's learning experiences in order for them to help facilitate the development process of their children as knowledge constructors. Working to connect families in this way can create coherence and continuity in the learning process and construct meaningful learning experiences for students.

Peg used Skype (https://www.skype.com) to engage families and the community with her classroom:

> Families become engaged when we Skype in the evenings. It builds excitement within the families and encourages them to try Skyping with others. Also, with all the digital resources and technology we use, the parents are excited and curious what their child is learning and how they are learning it. Our class has Skyped to join an administrative meeting to discuss blended education as well as Skyped with other classrooms in our district. OneNote (onenote.com) for classroom use helps the parents stay engaged in their student's learning and offers them a resource when I am not around to answer questions.

Technology can be used as a mechanism to connect families to many aspects of their children's in-class learning experiences. At the same time, technology can also offer a way for families to make contributions to their child's academic development. Joyce Epstein created a framework of six types of family involvement in school-related activities for their children: Parenting, Communicating, Volunteering, Learning at Home, Decision Making, and Collaborating with the Community. Technology and media tools can help to facilitate all six types of family involvement (Epstein, Coates, Salinas, Sanders, and Simon, 1997).

Table 3.1 provides a variety of activities that teachers can use to involve families and suggests specific apps, websites, and media that can be leveraged to do so, using Epstein's framework as a guide.

Table 3.1 Ways to Involve Families with the Use of Digital Media

Family Involvement Type	Description of Involvement Type	Suggested Technology Tools and Media
Parenting	This involves collaborating with families to provide information on anything that would assist in establishing home environments that support the development and well-being of children.	**Health and fitness:** Teachers can provide weekly suggestions on physical activities and exercises that students can do at home through interactive videos and games. **GoNoodle** (https://www.gonoodle.com)
Communicating	Regular two-way communication with families must occur, so that families have a way to communicate with schools and schools have a way to communicate with families.	**Sending and receiving messages**: Teachers can use the Remind app to send reminders, announcements, and other information to parents via cell phone or email. Remind also allows parents to send safe messages to teachers, without having to share personal cell phone numbers. Remind can send pictures and videos, which can be helpful for providing parents with real-time photos of their children in action at school. **Remind** (https://www.remind.com) **Arranging conferences:** Doodle provides a way for families to share the times they are available to meet for conferences, so that teachers are not simply giving them a time slot that may or may not work with their schedules. This shows families that teachers have a mutual respect for their time. **Doodle** (https://beta.doodle.com)
Volunteering	Schools must recruit volunteers and organize volunteer activities so that families take part in some aspect of the school experience outside of the learning that takes place in the home.	**Recruiting and organizing family volunteers:** It can be difficult to organize family volunteers and match them up with the time slot and activity that best meets their availability and interest. A technology tool such as Sign-Up Genius can help ameliorate these issues. **SignUpGenius** (signupgenius.com)

(continued on next page)

(continued from previous page)

Family Involvement Type	Description of Involvement Type	Suggested Technology Tools and Media
Learning at Home	Learning does not take place just in the classroom. There are many opportunities for learning while students are in the community and at home.	**Reading, numeracy, and critical thinking skills development:** Many websites and apps have a robust collection of learning activities in the areas of reading, literature, mathematics, and critical thinking. Teachers can send families links to specific content areas that students are working on in school and encourage that a blended learning setting is created at home. **PBS Parents** (pbs.org/parents/education) **ABCMouse.com** (https://www.abcmouse.com) **ChessKid** (https://www.chesskid.com)
Decision Making	Schools should involve families in decisions and families should serve in leadership roles to provide a voice for families and students.	**Advocacy mediums:** If allowed in the school's acceptable use policy, teachers can use Twitter to show families that their voices should and can be heard and provide various hashtags on issues related to their children's learning experiences. For example, with new policy changes such as the Every Student Succeeds Act (ESSA), families can be given the #ESSA hashtag to follow and contribute to the discussion. **Twitter** (www.twitter.com)
Collaborating with the Community	Family involvement includes working with the surrounding community to support their children's development and growth.	**Share writing and receive feedback:** Students write stories with families, type at home or at school, and then families and the class read and comment. **Storybird** (https://storybird.com)

Open connections among families, school, and the wider community benefit young learners, supporting and encouraging learning as a vital part of children's lives. The more we create caring communities and family-friendly schools, the more families, schools, and communities can develop effective partnerships (Couchenour & Chrisman, 2014), which will further support the development and growth of young learners.

Tools to Communicate with Families

In addition to using technology to facilitate family involvement through the six types of involvement as identified by Epstein (1996), teachers can effectively use technology to share learning with families in a variety of ways:

Classroom websites: Teachers can create classroom websites to post announcements, information, and photos of students while learning. A classroom website enables families to know what's going on in the lives of their children while at school.

Wix (https://www.wix.com), Weebly (https://www.weebly.com), and Google Sites (https://sites.google.com) are great tools with free options and templates that enable teachers to create attractive websites even if they don't have strong website building skills.

Shared Wikis: Wikis can be used to create a shared, collaborative space where families and teachers can add content. A shared wiki provides families a dedicated outlet to ask questions and post pictures and creative works that children are making at home. Teachers can also contribute to the wiki by sharing with parents some of the activities and exercises students are participating in at school. The goal of a shared wiki is joint ownership between families and teachers

Padlet: Padlet is a mobile technology that allows users to create a digital canvas or bulletin board for just about anything. Some popular uses are collecting content collaboratively and displaying and sharing the Padlet with various audiences. Teachers can use Padlets with families to house major assignments and parents can pose questions that teachers respond to right on the Padlet. Padlet can also be a hub for homework where teachers post instructions, sample completed assignments, FAQs, and links to learning videos. Having access to Padlet at home would benefit parents who may have questions in the evening but no access to an immediate response from teachers.

Private YouTube channel: Teachers can create a private YouTube channel that can be accessed by students and their families only. The teacher's private channel can house videos that document in-class learning and allow families to see exactly what learning experiences their children are having. Teachers can also post videos in which they explain a difficult concept or demonstrate how to do something. These videos can be extremely helpful for families and children during the evening when they are working on homework assignments and can contribute to increasing the number of students who successfully complete their homework.

Tools That Provide Personalized Feedback for Parents

Because families need a way to stay abreast on what their children are learning, several technology tools have emerged that provide them with personalized feedback regarding their children's development. Here are a few that we recommend:

Kaizena (https://kaizena.com): Kaizena is an app that allows teachers to talk to students and families about specific projects and papers, directly on students' work. It includes the ability to track progress by viewing and comparing feedback history over multiple assignments. Notifications will come when the family has responded to the comments. Kaizena also has Google integration features. An alternative to Kaizena is **Turnitin** (turnitin.com)

Jing (www.techsmith.com/jing.html): Jing enables teachers to create free short screencasts explaining a concept or demonstrating something. For example, a family member may email the teacher asking about the preferred method of answering a problem. In response, the teacher can create a Jing demonstrating the correct concept and email the link to parents to watch. And if families are having trouble logging in to the family portal that holds students' progress reports, teachers can use Jing to demonstrate how to log in. An alternative to Jing is **Screencast-O-Matic** (screencast-o-matic.com).

ShowMe (www.showme.com): ShowMe Interactive Whiteboard is an iPad app that enables teachers to create videos that they may then share, publicly or privately, on the ShowMe website. The videos shared by teachers can support students in their learning, especially when teachers are not available. Families may be able to watch the videos on ShowMe to get help with a concept they are working on with their children. An alternative to ShowMe is **Voki** (voki.com/teach/home).

Zoom (https://zoom.us): Is a free online conferencing tool that has screen sharing capabilities. Teachers may consider holding virtual office hours in the evenings to meet with families so they can discuss any issues they are having with helping their children with assignments. An alternative to Zoom is **GoToMeeting** (https://www.gotomeeting.com).

There are also a variety of specific apps that families can use to help their children develop their skills at home. Evening, weekend, and extended school breaks provide ideal times for children who may already be engaged with technology to work on their skills using a home computer or mobile device. You can find a list of a few suggested apps and software programs and their features on our wiki page (nurturingyounginnovators.wikispaces.com).

Supporting Families in Fostering Innovation in Children

While technology can help build connections, community building needs to meet families where they are. For example, some families may not be comfortable with the use of technology or they may prefer other means of communication. Just as we as teachers differentiate and meet the needs of our individual students, we need to do the same with families, and ensure we are culturally responsive by being sensitive and aware of their cultures and life experiences.

Alyssa and her students host monthly events to capture what they are studying. Alyssa also invites community members into her classroom to speak to students about their careers. Many of these community members have experienced great difficulties in life and are great examples of resilience and persistence for children and families:

> We reach out to the community to foster the sense of competency for my young learners. So far, we have asked a councilman to come speak to students and we are working on additional members of the community, such as doctors and lawyers. I want my students to see as large a variety of careers as possible, and I reach out to community members who overcame great odds to reach their goals.

The Centers for Disease Control and Prevention (CDC) (2012) reported:

> Engaging parents in their children's and adolescents' school life is a promising protective factor. Research shows that parent engagement in schools is closely linked to better student behavior, higher academic achievement, and enhanced social skills. Parent engagement also makes it more likely that children and adolescents will avoid unhealthy behaviors, such as tobacco, alcohol, and other drug use. (p. 6)

When we are working with families, we want to be sensitive to the factors that may be causing stress in their lives, and if possible, provide resources or support to families regarding their issue. Hosting family and community events that are fun, stress-free, and energizing help to build community and promote communication and collaboration. The CDC (2012) recommended schools "host events that provide information to parents on how the school works and how the school and parents can work together to promote the learning and health of their children" (p. 21).

Figure 3.1 illustrates a family and community event that our graduate education students planned and implemented to bring together family, school, and community. At the event, community organizations were available to provide information and support to families. We also held a science night bringing together family, community, and students (Figure 3.2). This event encouraged family and community collaboration while engaging families and students in learning. The CDC (2012) has stated that "by working with community organizations, schools can help parents obtain useful information and resources from these organizations and give parents access to community programs, services, and resources" (p. 18). The Community Connections example we share in this chapter is written by two social workers who have extensive experience working with families experiencing stress and challenging times. They provide ideas on how we all can support children and families, and how providing young children with creative activities can help channel some of the stress the children may be feeling in a positive direction. (Please see Appendix A for more resources to support families.)

Supporting Family Technology Access and Use

While the use of technology in homes has increased over the last few decades, not all families will be able to access the internet. According to the Educator Standards, teachers are called to "advocate for equitable access to educational technology, digital content and learning opportunities to meet the diverse needs of all students" (ISTE, 2017). We suggest ways to advocate and support families in accessing technology and digital content.

There are costs associated with using the internet at home, and even if there is free internet service, families may not have an available device to access it. In a recent study, the Pew Research

Figure 3.1 Family and community events can help support families by providing resources and access to community agencies.

Figure 3.2 A family and community event sponsoring science activities helped to bring families together and engage students in science learning with their families.

Community Connections

Providing Space for Grief

Rina Keller, MPA, MSS, LSW

Beth O'Rourke, MSW, LCSW, HSV

Loss exists on a continuum, and for younger students, may include a sibling leaving for college, military deployment of a parent, incarceration of a family member, separation and divorce of their parents, and/or the death of a close family member (including animal companions). Students who experience these losses and subsequent household reconfiguration may benefit from the opportunity to share their experiences, in school, in a safe and caring environment. Teachers who work with children who are experiencing loss—sudden, anticipated, short, or prolonged—should provide students with additional sensitivity and space to grieve. Attending school and engaging in their typical routine and structured educational activities, while also utilizing additional support where indicated, can help students begin processing their grief while exploring life following the loss, thus allowing them to begin creating a new normal. Teachers should make an effort to support the family, employ school resources to provide children with additional care, and seek to validate and empower the child.

Where possible, teachers, social workers, and other school professionals may choose to attend important family events, including viewings or funerals, in order to show their commitment to supporting the student and the family. Emotions around significant dates including anniversaries, birthdays, and holidays are generally heightened and, for children who are experiencing loss, are often further intensified. Communicating regularly with the child's family to discuss home and school behavior is useful in order to monitor the child's grieving process and needs. Often, children will react to their grief in different ways depending on the setting. Questions to ask caregivers include: How is the child dealing with the grief at home? Does he or she talk about it? Is the child resuming regular activities and behavior or isolating himself or herself? In many cases, children feel pressure (real or perceived) to behave in a particular way at home, and therefore allowing them a safe space in school to grieve, without the added burden of familial expectations, helps their overall functioning. Teachers should monitor the student's attendance, behavior, and grades so that additional academic and/or mental health support can be offered as needed. School social workers or counselors can also offer the student and family information about other community resources including therapy and support groups.

(continued on next page)

(continued from previous page)

Teachers should utilize school staff, such as social workers, counselors, and psychologists, and request support for the student in the form of one-on-one time and/or small group activities that will provide the grieving child a calm space to share while receiving more individualized attention. If a student does not initially engage, teachers are encouraged to continue to offer support. Some children may want to keep their grief private; others may take some time to open up. A brief chat or creative activity is recommended in order for the child to honor the person or relationship that has changed, while also recognizing his or her own strengths in living with and through the experience. The exact activity depends on the specific child and the child's developmental stage. Some students simply want to talk, and professionals should listen and answer questions while being careful not to compare or minimize any loss, as every person grieves differently. Conversation prompts may include questions about the situation or person they have lost and particular memories that come to mind. Creative activities for preserving memories include storytelling, drawing, journaling, or looking at pictures. Channeling their grief during conversations with caring professionals or while participating in creative activities helps to provide children with the space, without correction or redirection, to process their loss.

Teachers, social workers, and other school professionals should seek primarily to validate a child's feelings and not necessarily to provide a "fix." Children should be allowed time to feel, as they need to learn to both experience and control a myriad of emotions in healthy ways. Support staff should assist students in identifying all of their available resources in school (friends, teachers), at home (family, friends, neighbors), and in the community (church, sports teams). At a time when the loss and ensuing grief may make a child feel out of control, empowering the student by providing an opportunity for them to decide how they want to utilize the support time provided at school will assist them in building self-efficacy, even during a time of bereavement.

Center found that 13% of adults in America do not use the internet (Anderson & Perrin, 2016). Additionally, there has been shown to be a digital divide between minorities and their Caucasian counterparts in how the internet is used and the levels of internet access available (Boone, Hendricks, & Waller, 2014). Here, we suggest several things that can be done to provide families with resources for obtaining internet access, a requirement for continuing to learn at home in the technologically impacted environment of the digital age.

Considering Accessibility of Technology for Families

Not all families have access to a computer at home, and some will use their cell phones to access the internet. Because of this, if sending home electronic forms to be completed, try to use mobile-friendly applications. For example, Google Forms will allow for ease of use on cell phones and has an accompanying mobile app. Computer usage hubs should also be provided in and by schools at times when families can use the computers or similar devices to complete electronic forms. The U.S. government also has several programs, such as SafeLink Wireless (goo.gl/xE2hx0), that provide free smart phones to families who meet certain income guidelines.

It is important to provide resources to families who need help getting internet access. Many school districts and cities have programs centered around providing students with internet access outside of the school day. The Peninsula School District in Bay Harbor, Washington, works with a variety of organizations to provide free Wi-Fi to students and provides a map of their free Wi-Fi directory (https://psd401.net/free-student-wifi-directory). Following are a few programs that provide free and low-cost internet and are designed specifically to help low-income families get internet access at home (content from their websites):

Comcast Internet Essentials Program (goo.gl/cUJ9f2): Families can obtain low-cost internet service as well as computer equipment at a discounted price if at least one child is eligible to participate in the national school lunch program.

Access from AT&T (https://www.att.com/shop/internet/access/#/): Families can obtain low-cost internet service if they qualify. The web link above provides the qualification details for families.

Google: Google funded a grant program that provides students with laptops and free Wi-Fi to complete their homework on their long bus ride to and from school. The population targeted for this grant opportunity through Google was a rural area in South Carolina where internet access is limited. Google hopes to expand grant opportunities to other rural areas in the future. (Kinnard, 2017)

Family Technology Checklist

Before you create projects for students to work on both at home and in school, we suggest providing each family with a technology checklist to assess the resources they have available to them at home and their comfort level with technology. The checklist can be done through Google Forms (https://docs.google.com/forms/u/0) or physical copies of the checklist can be provided. Based on the results of these checklists, you should adapt homework assignments accordingly or provide families with the proper resources needed for students to complete the assignments at home. Here are some items to include on the checklist:

Hardware/Equipment

- I have access to a computer in the household.
- I have access to a tablet in the household.
- I have access to a mobile phone in the household.
- I have access to a video camera (can be on phone, tablet, or computer) in the household.
- I have access to a camera that takes photographs in the household.
- I have access to audio speakers or headphones in the household.

Internet Access

- I have access to the internet on a computer in the household.
- I have access to the internet on a tablet in the household.
- I have access to the internet on a mobile phone in the household.

Makerspace Tools

- I have expired or working batteries in the household.
- I have string in the household.
- I have scrap cardboard in the household.
- I have recycled tin or metal in the household.
- I have scrap paper in the household.
- I have tape or glue in the household.

Comfort Level with Technology Tools

- I am very comfortable with technology tools.
- I am somewhat comfortable with technology tools.
- I am not comfortable with technology tools.

Project to Connect Schools, Families, and the Community

This project can be used for all grade levels.

A community walk/video slideshow integrates technology and shares highlights in a community. This activity demonstrates the importance of the home, school and community connections we have discussed throughout this chapter.

If Doing This... Why Not Try This? ❯❯❯

Genealogy Interviews: If having students interview a family member to gather genealogy information

Audio or Video Record Genealogy Interviews: Instead of having students write the responses of an interview with an elder family member, have them audio or video record the interviews. The recorded interviews will allow for a more detailed recollection of the interview contents, and students can show them to their classmates and teachers.

Creating a Recipe: If encouraging students to create their own recipes connecting to a content area they're focusing on in class

Family Cooking Night: Have students bring home the recipes they created at school and try to make them their families. Connect the assignment to health or science class, and provide families with a template they can use to track nutritional value and that the children can use to monitor that all of the food groups are included in their recipes.

Planet Assignment: If assigning students a planet to create at home out of cardboard and other materials

3D Planet Assignment: Have students use a home makerspace area consisting of commonly found household products, and create a 3D planet of their choice. As an alternative, have students design their own planet that they bring to school to print on a 3D printer, if available.

Researching a Historic Figure: If having students locate five facts about a historic figure (Dr. Martin Luther King Jr., President Abraham Lincoln, etc.)

Historic Figure for a Day: Assign students to research a historic figure and learn about that person and some of the contributions he or she has made. Then have each student come to school dressed like the historic figure and "be" that historic figure for the day.

Description of community walk/video slideshow: The educational experience of children is impacted by the community in which they live. It's important for you to intimately get to know the community you are teaching in, especially if you do not live within that community. In this group/class assignment, the class goes on a community walk and takes pictures, then creates a digital slideshow of their community. The children can be involved in taking pictures and creating the slideshow.

Alternative idea to engage family: This community walk/video slideshow can be done as a take-home assignment in which families create their own community walk/video slideshows and then share their videos on the school's website. Or, children can also present their families' slideshows in class.

Requirements:

- Spend a few hours walking in the community.
- Go inside as many establishments as possible.
- Take pictures and make videos of what you see.
- Put together a slideshow using any application or technology tool of your choice.
- Make sure the slideshow using your pictures, videos, and captions tells a story.
- At the end of your slideshow, include a reflection (video or slide) on the community and its impact on children.

+ Reflection Questions

Here are some questions to consider after you've completed this chapter:

- In what ways do you keep connections open between the home, school, and the community?
- How do you accommodate families whose first language is not English?
- What kind of technology do you use, or would you use, to effectively communicate with families and why?
- How can families and teachers work together to assist children in building their capacity to use a variety of technology and media tools?
- How can you ensure your students' families have access to technology and, if they do not, how can you support them in getting access?
- Because not all families have access to a computer, remember to consider mobile-friendly apps. What kind of mobile-friendly apps do you use to communicate with families?
- What kind of community resources are available to help enrich and support families and young learners? How do you share this information with families?
- How can you engage mentors, businesses, and community volunteers in helping to support young learners and families?

Encouraging Choice to Improve Student Learning

"You can't use up creativity. The more you use, the more you have."

—Maya Angelou

Providing young students with assessments and choices in their learning that are meaningful to them encourages them to be engaged learners. Thompson and Beymer (2015) stated, "Offering choice in the classroom is one way to increase student motivation by appealing to students' needs for autonomy and competence" (p. 105). Encouraging students to explore their passions and allotting classroom time for this reflective process and inquiry will lead to transformative and deeper learning. Intrinsic motivation comes alive when students are able to explore topics that are of interest to them (Thompson & Beymer, 2015). According to the ISTE Standards for Educators, the teacher acts as facilitator of learning and encourages "a culture where students take ownership of their learning goals and outcomes in both independent and group settings." (International Society for Technology in Education [ISTE], 2017)

Chapter Overview

This chapter will cover the following:

- Supporting students as creative communicators
- Ideas for encouraging choice to motivate students
- Letting students explore their passions through a "genius hour"
- Helping young learners develop a growth mindset
- The role of play in nurturing autonomous and confident learners
- Supporting an atmosphere of choice through Universal Design for Learning (UDL)

- Using choice boards to enhance student learning
- Reducing stress by allowing choice
- Reflection questions specific to igniting passion and excitement

Student as Creative Communicator

"Students communicate clearly and express themselves creatively for a variety of purposes using the platforms, tools, styles, formats and digital media appropriate for their goals."

— *ISTE Standards for Students, Standard 6: Creative Communicator*

Adults can help encourage children to be creative communicators by allowing them opportunities to make informed choices and giving them time to communicate their ideas with others. Part of being a creative communicator is also knowing how to choose the appropriate tools to use. Young learners need exposure to a variety of tools and methods for expressing their creativity through digital media.

Throughout this chapter, we explore and discuss ways to support childrens' personalized learning and provide opportunities for them to make informed choices.

Freedom to Choose, Create, and Innovate

The U.S. Department of Education and Office of Educational Technology (2017) reported that technology is being used to personalize learning, allowing children to choose "what and how they learn and at what pace" (p. 7), and that this also helps to develop lifelong learners who enjoy learning. Duncan and Salcedo (2015) explained

Children's minds are confined when they are not allowed to make choices, think on their own, or consider the many ways a problem could be solved. When children are limited to mundane tasks or experiences (i.e., project art, flashcards or letters of the week), they are cheated out of opportunities to truly engage their minds. (p. 27)

So not only should young learners be provided choices, but adults in their lives can facilitate activities where children can choose and then have time to think about and discuss their choices. Accordingly, the Educator Standards suggested that teachers "use technology to create, adapt and personalize learning experiences that foster independent learning and accommodate learner differences and needs" (ISTE, 2017). Learning to think about thinking (metacognition) is an important part of innovation and creativity. Metacognition helps children to learn how to problem solve (Strimel, 2014). Boyle, Butler, and Li (2017) shared the following insight: "If we want our children to slow down and notice to wonder, if we want them to love and stay with the challenges that they find for themselves in the smallest of things, then we need to do this too" (p. 54). There are many ways adults working with young children can offer choices in the classroom, home, and the community.

Thompson and Beymer (2015) provided the following suggestions for offering choices:

- Allow students to choose their due date on assignments—this option allows them to work at their own pace.
- Provide students with options for assignments, so that they choose which one they want to complete. (This can be on a choice board that lists the assignment choices like a Tic-Tac-Toe board or a Dinner Menu board; examples are provided later in this chapter.)
- Have students choose their own groups and who they will work with for a particular assignment or activity.
- Allow students to choose their own research topics (for example, in genius hour, students can focus on their passion and interest).

Allowing children to choose helps them to become autonomous and builds their self-esteem (Grossman, n.d.). When children are young, simple activities like choosing where to sit or what kind of materials to collect all lead to helping them become autonomous and persistent in learning. Grossman (n.d.) noted that "a child who has a solid sense of self-worth can make a poor decision, evaluate it calmly, rethink the situation, and make a different choice" (para. 7). As we discussed in Chapter 2, it's important to create an environment that supports risk-taking, and allowing choice and embracing mistakes will help learners take the risks that can ultimately lead to creativity and innovation.

Allowing Choice Through Flexible Seating

Delzer (2016) shared the following benefits of using flexible seating in the classroom: "burning more calories, using up excess energy, improving metabolism, increased motivation and engagement, creating a better oxygen flow to the brain, and improving core strength and overall posture" (para. 3). When requesting

Figure 4.1 Children in a second-grade classroom have the choice to sit on an exercise ball while learning. Photo credit: Loren Loomis

Figure 4.2 Balance ball chairs can be effective in any classroom, but especially for learners who may need sensory support or learners with ADD/ADHD. These balance balls also have wheels so that students can move around in them. Photo credit: MaryBeth and Maria Cheeseman

Figure 4.3 Wobble chairs allow learners to move around while sitting in one place. Photo credit: MaryBeth and Maria Cheeseman.

Figure 4.4 Beanbags provide an affordable way for teachers to include flexible seating in their classroom. They create a comfortable atmosphere for learners who prefer this type of seating. Photo credit: MaryBeth and Maria Cheeseman

stories and photos from teachers on social media, we received a few examples of redesigned classrooms with flexible seating (Figures 4.1 through 4.4). Loren shared the following observation about flexible seating: "It is a more comfortable environment that helps my students be their best learning selves. It gives my students a sense of ownership to their education."

Peg shared another way she allows choice in her classroom with flexible seating:

> In second grade, I use flexible seating (balls, bouncy bands, pillows, beanbags, stools, drafting tables, floor tables, etc.). The main guideline in our classroom is that you are responsible for your learning and the learning of your peers. We go back to that almost daily. I let [students] sit where they want and give them freedom when learning.

Creative Ideas to Encourage Choice

In Chapter 1, we shared an example in which Helene took her young children to a fairy garden. During this visit to the garden, Helene allowed the children to journal (draw pictures) about the fairy houses they found. She encouraged them to discuss their journal entries with each other, and then gather materials outside and create their own fairy garden. This activity was open-ended but with the goal of having the children refer back to their journals (thinking about their own thinking), involve their families in their projects, and make choices on their own to find materials to create their fairy garden. The activity demonstrates imagination, creativity, and innovation, because the children had to imagine the kind of house they would want for their fairy, decide on the materials they would use, and then create it.

Figure 4.5 After visiting a fairy garden, the children were asked to create one. They went on a nature walk and chose any outdoor materials they found that they wanted to use for their fairy house creation. Photo credit: Helene McLaughlin McKelvey

This is also a great example of how to support children as creative communicators. The children could create videos in which they share their creations and talk about why they chose the materials they used for their fairy houses and how they went about creating them. They could be asked to create multimedia presentations combining some or all of the following: photographs, sound, text, video, narration, or pictures they drew of the fairies that would live in their houses. Figures 4.5 and 4.6 illustrate the children working on their fairy house creations. As Grossman (n.d.) pointed out, "making choices is part of problem solving. When given choices, children stretch their minds and create new and unique combinations of ideas and materials" (para. 9).

Figure 4.6 Families can contribute to helping children create and innovate by providing them with open-ended activities that are of interest to them. The children were interested in fairies and were provided time to notice and wonder and then create. Photo credit: Helene McLaughlin McKelvey

Learning before Tools

When we offer lists of tools or resources to use with young children, it is important to note that we never focus on the tool first. Instead, we focus on the learning first and then decide if the tool would work. Rich and Lavallee (2017) offered the following tips:

- Choose the learning goal first and then decide on the tool.
- Choose media that fosters children's learning.
- Choose media that encourages interaction. (pp. 150–153)

Peg shared ways she uses technology in her classroom to provide variety and allow students to make choices:

> In our second-grade classroom we have a mini lab of desktop computers, laptops, surface tablets, and iPads. I encourage BYOD (Bring Your Own Device), so children will bring in Chromebooks, tablets, and additional iPads. We have a Makey Makey for coding and exploring. We have several cameras for Skyping and headphones with microphones. We also have the common technology of ELMOS and interactive white-boards that we use during whole group activities. We use several digital resources and some adaptive digital curriculum programs daily.

There are numerous digital tools available for supporting choice and personalized learning in your class. The following list suggest a few these tools.

Digital Tools to Support Personalized Learning

- **Classkick**—This app provides a way to give real-time and instant feed-back to students; students can also give feedback to each other.
- **Evernote**—Teachers and students can use this app to collect and share ideas across devices.
- **Educreations**—Users create videos by importing their content and recording their voice and iPad screen. They can then share their videos instantly.
- **Kidblog**—With this tool, students can publish their writing online and share classroom activities with their families.
- **Google Docs**—The class can use Google Docs to create, edit, and share work online.
- **Nearpod**—This tool allows you to take students on virtual field trips.

- **Spacedeck**—This tool provides a place to post, share, and access resources and ideas.
- **VoiceThread**—With this cloud application, users can share media and then comment using audio, text, or video.
- **Wikispaces for Educators**—From this site, you can create a place to share ideas and allow students and families to communicate.

Let Passion Lead Learning with Genius Hour

Businesses like Google have been using "genius hour" for years to encourage their employees to think creatively and to innovate. More recently, schools have followed suit, integrating this idea into the classroom to encourage creativity and innovation. Matteson (2016) explained that genius hour is "different everywhere" but consists of "a time set aside for students to work on and learn about what interests them most" (p. 37). Joy Kirr provides a LiveBinder, titled "Genius Hour / 20% Time" (https://t.co/rmH6P9bEhi), with a multitude of resources to help you get started implementing genius hour in your class or to support what you are already doing.

During genius hour, students are given a block of time to explore their passions, interests, and things they wonder about. Kessler (2013) described genius hour as "a movement that allows students to explore their own passions and encourages creativity in the classroom. It provides students a choice in what they learn during a set period during school" (p. 1). In the early years, we suggest working as a group when first exploring genius hour with young children; as they obtain more confidence, they can then explore on their own. Also, instead of leaving options completely open for the child or group to decide on, here are some specific ideas to use with younger children:

- Make a video on a specific interest topic.
- Plant a garden.
- Create something with wood and other woodworking materials.
- Collect rocks, then display and explain the collection.

The hope is that children will be excited about learning and want to continue learning when outside of the classroom. Inviting families into the classroom to discuss their passions and careers will provide children with various topics that may interest them and helps to connect the families to the school and the community. Community members can also be invited to share their passions and ideas with the children.

Here are some ideas for igniting student passions with genius hour; these can be modified depending on the age and needs of the children:

Ask students to brainstorm topics they are passionate about. You can do this on a classroom bulletin board with sticky notes or digitally with software like Padlet or Lino (Letter, 2016). On the Wonder Wall, write each student's name and make a list beneath each name of the topics that child most wonders about and wants to know more about. From this list, eventually, students can choose the one topic to focus on. Kirr (2017) has provided multiple examples of brainstorming and using prompts such as "I Wonder...," (Figure 4.7), "I'm a Genius when it comes to ...," or "If I could create a new class, it would be called..." on her blog post "Half Year Mark" (http://geniushour.blogspot.com/2013/01/half-year-mark.html).

Create a space where students can collect questions about the topic they are interested in. This is similar to the Wonder Wall, except students go beyond sharing topics to sharing questions about the topics they are passionate about. We suggest using Google Docs, Padlet, or the school's learning management system as ways to create a collaborative space for students to place these questions. Kyritsis (2014) explained the difference between a "Googleable" and a "Non-Googleable" question in her blog post "Genius Hour" (elenikyritsis.com/2014/08/27/genius -hour). For genius hour, students' questions should not be able to be answered with a simple Google search; students need to dig deeper to find the answers.

Provide time for students to do research each week. Within the classroom, you can set up stations with students rotating among each one. One station can be a computer station, another can be a place to create and make, and another can be a place for students to talk and collaborate with their classmates and teacher about their ideas.

Ask students to record their stories and share their passions and plans. This task can lead students to the next stage of creating and innovating.

Have students share their completed project. Students can share their passions on a class website, or, if appropriate, they can share with the larger community on social media, such as on Facebook or Twitter.

Shannon Brace shared an example of how she incorporates genius hour and a growth mindset in her teaching. Shannon has her students reflect on the failures that happened during genius hour (Figure 4.8). Acknowledging failure is part of the process and an excellent way to encourage children to have a growth mindset.

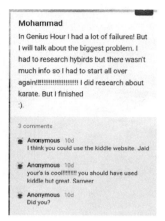

Figure 4.7 On her blog post, Joy Kirr shared this bulletin board displaying what students wonder about. Some of their responses included "How stop motions were invented," "About the history of teddy bears," and "If everybody in the world made their dreams come true, how different the world would be."

Figure 4.8 Shannon Brace shared her 8- and 9-year-old students' reflections related to genius hour failures. Classmates provided each other with encouragement or tips regarding their failures.

Her "Genius Hour Failures" Padlet page (https://padlet.com/SBrace/geniushourfailures) includes the students' reflections and their classmates' responses.

The many examples shared by Joy and Shannon demonstrate the Educator Standards in that teachers are called to "design authentic learning activities that align with content area standards and use digital tools and resources to maximize active, deep learning" (ISTE, 2017). The students are engaged and passionate about topics they have chosen and are able to share their learning with others, but only because their teachers have facilitated these authentic learning activities.

Play, Choice, and Social Development

Ensuring that learners are developing in all aspects of their life, including socially, is essential. As discussed in Chapter 2, play is a natural way to support children to take risks and try out new ways of learning, but play is also necessary when it comes to helping children become autonomous and confident learners. Young learners need opportunities to have hands-on experiences, and interacting with others socially through play within the classroom helps children to develop creativity and innovation skills. Isenberg and Jalongo (2014) explained the value of play to support learning:

Play supports children's learning in two main ways. First, it helps children learn knowledge, skills, and dispositions—such as problem solving, perseverance, and self-regulation—that are essential for learning and school success. Second, play serves as a vehicle for learning other skills such as language, literacy and social skills. (p. 46)

Figure 4.9 The dramatic play area allows children to explore choices that encourage their creativity and social development. For example, children can dress up as doctors or community workers to extend a social studies lesson.

Figure 4.10 Setting up classrooms with real-life props helps children to make choices while playing and also develop critical social skills needed in everyday life. Photo credit: Carolyn Stillman

The dramatic play area supplies endless ways to nurture young innovators (Figures 4.9 and 4.10). Young children often learn critical life skills from their social interactions in the classroom. For example, "play supports children's emotional development by providing a way for them to express and manage both positive and negative feelings" (Isenberg & Jalongo, 2014, p. 59). Technology can help to create a classroom environment that is warm and inclusive and that enables pro-social behavior. When children have access to technology tools to support their learning, they can make choices as they play (Isenberg & Jalongo, 2014). The integration of active play with technology can further support students as creative communicators.

An example of active play with the use of technology is the app GooseChase (available for iOS and Android). Teachers can set up a scavenger hunt game with specific missions for young children to accomplish in teams (Figure 4.11). While working with our preservice teachers on leadership skills, we created a GooseChase challenge for second graders visiting our university. We played the game in groups of twenty-five with five on a team and one team leader (who was a preservice teacher). The game encouraged the students to be social and active, and when they came back after completing the missions, the missions were shared on interactive whiteboards with everyone. The game can be played with a variety of grade levels and is even good for professional development. The missions can change to fit the content area or focus of the event (Figure 4.12).

Another example of using technology to engage children in social activities and making choices is Social Adventures. This app helps children ages 5 and up think and learn and choose appropriate social skills. The Social Express II app, for children ages 8 and up, provides social adventures through animated lessons. And

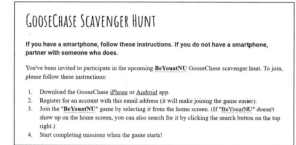

Figure 4.11 Students can collaborate with one another in a GooseChase scavenger hunt. This activity can be modified for different grade levels and content areas. This game was used with preservice teachers and with second graders who were visiting our university and learning about leadership skills.

Figure 4.12 The free version of GooseChase allows for five teams, and we chose team leaders who would lead the second graders on their missions. The app allows for children to make choices on how to accomplish their missions, and encourages creativity, innovation, collaboration, and communication.

to help children ages 6 and up build global awareness, One Globe Kids includes stories about children from around the world. The kinds of personal interactions and play experiences children can have with these apps are critical in helping them to develop and grow as creative communicators.

Helping Young Learners Develop a Growth Mindset

The U.S. Department of Education and the Office of Educational Technology (2017) defined a growth mindset as "the understanding that abilities can be developed through effort and practice and [lead] to increased motivation and achievement" (p. 11). When we create child-centered classrooms led by student interests and passions, creativity and innovation can thrive. Families can also be supportive by encouraging a growth mindset when their children are home. Helping children develop a growth mindset is important for all learners, but especially early learners. Most children are curious and open and natural lovers of learning, and if we send them a fixed mindset message—that is, a belief that one's personality traits and intelligence cannot change or grow—they may lose confidence and their inherent excitement for learning. Coates (2013) provided the following information about the dangers of sending a fixed mindset message:

> Parents, caregivers, and teachers can send a fixed mindset message
> through their words, choices, decisions, actions, and behaviors,

> ultimately oppressing a child's natural curiosity and intrinsic motivation to "grow." For example, when we provide unnecessary help or support to children on a given task or activity that they can otherwise do independently we are restricting their natural desire to develop and "grow." We are sending the message: "You can't do it yourself, you need my help." (para. 5)

Although we all want what is best for young children in our care, the current structure of many schools can send a fixed mindset message when it comes to grades, right answers, one-size-fits-all approaches, and discouraging curiosity and questions (Coates, 2013).

In Chapter 2, we discussed the practice of focusing on the process over the product to encourage children to take risks. This mentality can help children continue trying to learn even if they do not succeed at first. Carol Dweck's 2014 TED Talk "The Power of Believing That You Can Improve" (tinyurl.com/NYI-Dwecktedtalk) also stresses the importance of helping students to develop a growth mindset: In the talk, Dweck provides the example of a high school that instead of failing students when they do not pass tests, grades them with "Not Yet." This action sends the message that although students didn't succeed at this time, they can eventually "get it." While this example is for high school, it is certainly transferable to any grade level. Praising the process that children engage in helps teach them to be resilient (Dweck, 2014), whereas focusing on the end product while children are struggling with learning something can be discouraging.

In Chapter 2, we provided examples of a risk-taking rubric that can be used to assess the process (tinyurl.com/NYI-risktakingrubric). This is particularly important when we are giving children choice, as this shift in focus can help students feel more freedom to try something they have not done before or that they find challenging. If a student is struggling with an area or a way of learning, allowing choice in when their assignment is due or what their topic of focus will be may help them succeed where they were not able to before. Therefore, teaching children how to think with a growth mindset can improve learning, motivation, and excitement in the classroom. The bulletin board in Loren's second-grade classroom reminds her students to have a growth mindset (Figure 4.13).

Figure 4.13 Bulletin board displays can help remind children to have a growth mindset as opposed to a fixed mindset. Photo credit: Loren Loomis

Peg shared how she encourages a growth mindset in her second-grade classroom:

> From day one, I encourage creative thinking by helping the children develop a growth mindset. In my classroom, all the students understand that they are self-learners and can learn anything they want to because they can take the initiative to learn and they have the resources to do it at school.

Finley (2014) provided teaching strategies to encourage a growth mindset:

- Teach children early on to set goals.
- Praise effort as opposed to praising intelligence.
- Stress the process over the product.
- Encourage children to work in groups and to collaborate on projects together.

Allowing Choice Through Universal Design for Learning

Harte (2013) defined Universal Design for Learning (UDL) as "a framework that helps educators to remove barriers and provide supports while also challenging students" (p. 18). UDL should provide learners with individual ways to demonstrate learning and participate in all activities. We suggest providing choice as a way to meet the individual needs of the students in the classroom. As stated in checkpoint 7.1 from the National Center on Universal Design for Learning (National UDL Center) Guidelines (2012), teachers should "optimize individual choice and autonomy." Later in this chapter we provide examples related to checkpoint 7.1, including a Tic-Tac-Toe choice board that allows students to choose the assignment they want to complete. Another example that illustrates how UDL optimizes individual choice and autonomy is to have students use Book Adventure (bookadventure.com) to choose from a variety of books to read.

According to the National UDL Center (2014), the following three principles guide UDL, and each includes multiple examples of choice:

I. Provide Multiple Means of Representation: Teachers should introduce and teach content in a variety of ways using different types of learning tools. In addition to verbally sharing the content with students, teachers should choose additional ways to share the information, such as these:

- Use visual aids.
- Have content on board using a projector.
- Provide picture examples.
- Demonstrate concepts through modeling.

II. Provide Multiple Means of Action and Expression: Students must have multiple ways to demonstrate their learning. Instead of having students answer questions through a unit test, some other choices students might have to demonstrate learning are:

- Write a persuasive essay.
- Create a multimedia presentation.
- Organize a portfolio.
- Act in a play.

III. Provide Multiple Means of Engagement: Students must be presented with different activities to help them meet the learning objectives. After students have been introduced to the content, allow them to choose a variety of ways to engage with the content. Some examples of other ways to engage with the content include the following:

- Work in peer learning teams.
- Complete guided notes sheets.
- Go to the interactive whiteboard and interact with learning activities.

Peg shared an example of how technology can support learners who have special needs:

We are currently working on finding the best dictation program to use for one of my students who is writing at a kindergarten level. I want her to be able to share all the stories and ideas she has without having to use only words that she knows how to write. This will create a much better representation of her storytelling skills. The other writing skills will still be worked on, but in the mean time she can feel successful and have something she can share independently with her peers. One great thing about digital learning is that some programs come in multiple languages, and if not, almost every device has some form of dictation/translation program that can be used with it.

Adults should ensure all children have what they need to learn. This means considering the environment, the materials, and the specific needs of the child and the family. If children are not able to learn due to a barrier, it affects their ability to be creative and innovative. As we've shown here, children need choices to help them learn.

Choice Boards

Choice boards provide children with options on what they will complete for a particular assessment. According to the Educator Standards, it is recommended to "provide alternative ways for students to demonstrate competency and reflect on their learning using technology" (ISTE, 2017). A few ways to offer children choice would be a Tic-Tac-Toe choice board or a Dinner Menu choice board. These choice boards can be modified and used with a variety of grade levels as long as the choices within the boards are appropriate to the particular age group. Also, these choice boards can be used for any content area and connected with national, state, or Common Core standards for the content area covered in the assessment.

Tic-Tac-Toe Choice Boards

The ultimate goal of providing choice is to motivate students and increase their learning. Tic-Tac-Toe choice boards provide a way for children to choose the assignments they will complete and, most importantly, those they are interested in. The assignments are also formative assessments and provide the teacher with information on the student's learning related to a specific content area. When using the Tic-Tac-Toe choice board, the teacher adds assignments that students can then choose from throughout a semester (it can be for a unit or for a year—this is up to the teacher). The assignments can be aligned with Blooms Taxonomy to provide a variety of choices at different levels. Teachers can ask students to choose as many assignments as they want them to complete. Typically, throughout a semester, a student would complete three assessments with the goal of getting Tic-Tac-Toe on their board—so, for example, it could be three down, three across, or three diagonal. The amount of assignments the student needs to complete can vary depending on the student's grade level and ability.

Primary Professional Development Services (n.d) shared the following about Tic-Tac-Toe choice boards:

> Tic-Tac-Toe boards complement a child-centered approach to learning, in that the student is motivated through the power of choice. Tic-Tac-Toe boards encourage independent learning using a structured approach and enable the teacher to provide controlled choices to the children in his/her class. (p. 18)

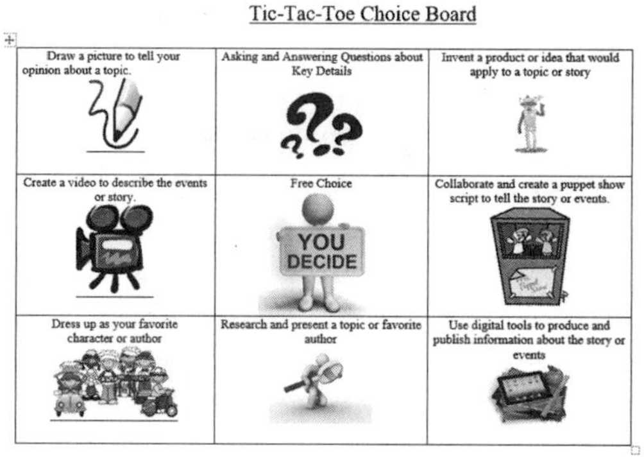

Tic-Tac-Toe Choice Board

Draw a picture to tell your opinion about a topic.	Asking and Answering Questions about Key Details	Invent a product or idea that would apply to a topic or story
Create a video to describe the events or story.	Free Choice YOU DECIDE	Collaborate and create a puppet show script to tell the story or events.
Dress up as your favorite character or author	Research and present a topic or favorite author	Use digital tools to produce and publish information about the story or events

Figure 4.14 Tic-Tac-Toe choice boards can provide students with choices related to assignments that in turn will help them to create and innovate.

The earlier you integrate choice with young children, the more comfortable they will be taking a risk and trying something new. We have worked with adult students who were never provided a choice of assessment until they were in one of our classes. By this time, it was challenging for the student to complete an assignment without being given a specific task to complete. The Tic-Tac-Toe menu requires children to think deeper, problem solve, and come up with a plan for how to get three in a row. We created a Tic-Tac-Toe choice board as an example that we aligned with Kindergarten Common Core State Standards (Figure 4.14). The blocks can be modified for other content areas, standards, and so on.

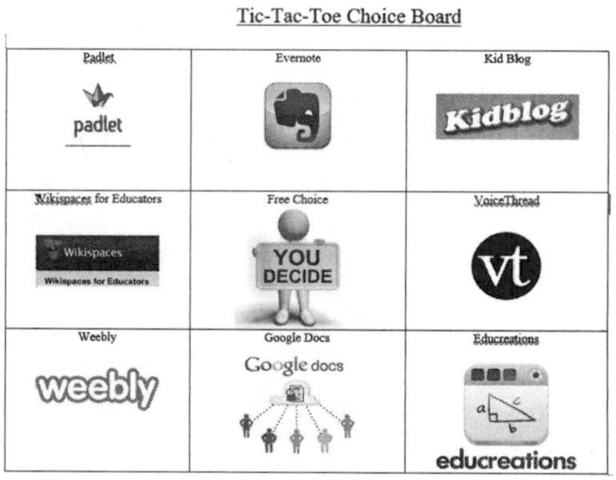

Tic-Tac-Toe Choice Board

Padlet padlet	Evernote	Kid Blog Kidblog
Wikispaces for Educators Wikispaces	Free Choice YOU DECIDE	VoiceThread vt
Weebly weebly	Google Docs Google docs	Educreations educreations

Figure 4.15 When teachers are convinced that choice helps motivate students to learn, they will integrate choice into the classroom. This Tic-Tac-Toe board provides teachers with choices on digital apps they can use.

Tic-Tac-Toe choice boards can also be used by teachers, during professional development or as part of a learning community, to encourage the use of different digital tools in the classroom. For example, teachers can decide on learning goals first, and then decide to try a digital tool that is new to them. This kind of interaction also helps teachers to stay connected and aware of up-to-date digital tools and resources and connects well to the Educator Standards, wherein teachers are called to be learners who "stay current with research that supports improved student learning outcomes, including findings from the learning sciences" (ISTE, 2017). Whitaker, Zoul, and Casas (2015) described connected educators "as ones who are actively and constantly seeking new opportunities and resources to grow as professionals" (p. xxiii). We created an example of a Tic-Tac-Toe choice board that could be used as described (Figure 4.15). Again, we do not focus on the tools, but on the learning goal. This Tic-Tac-Toe idea can be modified to reflect different digital tools, depending on the situation.

Dinner Menu Choice Board

Creating choice boards in a dinner menu style is another good way to allow choice for young children. The Dinner Menu choice board can include a variety of choices in the categories of appetizer, main dish, side dish, and dessert. For very young children, you can start out with a main dish that they can choose from. When children learn to choose their assignments, this teaches them problem solving, critical thinking, and planning skills. The students also self-assess their learning, and teachers can use this as a formative assessment to see what students have learned and what they still need to learn related to a particular content area. An example of how one of the authors provides choice using a Dinner Menu board is the Dinner Menu—Science Methods board (tinyurl.com/NYI-Dinnermenuexample). Figure 4.16 is a blank template for you to use to generate your own ideas; we also provide an example of what it would look like to offer young children a main menu choice only.

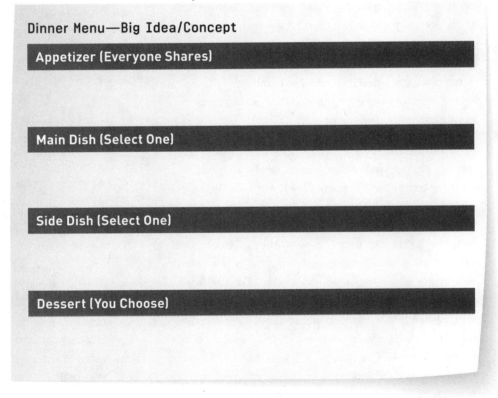

Figure 4.16 Providing students with a Dinner Menu choice board gives them a variety of options for assignments they can complete throughout the semester or unit. Teachers and/or students can then use this choice board to assess students' progress at the end of the semester or unit.

You can access this Dinner Menu choice board template on our wiki (http://nurturingyounginnovators.wikispaces.com/Resources).

We created an example of how to use the Dinner Menu choice board with younger children and connected it to the Next Generation Science Standards (NGSS) to demonstrate how this can easily be done (Figure 4.17). This Main Menu choice board is for first graders learning about waves, light, and sound. The standard addressed is NGSS 1-PS4-4: "Use tools and materials to design and build a device that uses light or sound to solve the problem of communicating over a distance." The children choose one option from the Main Menu and this is the assignment they will complete to meet this standard. You can modify the Main Menu options according to the topic you are covering and then relate them to whichever standards apply. The idea is that children will not all complete the same assignment, but will get to choose the one they each would like to complete. All three of the Main Menu activities demonstrate the same learning outcomes, but in a different way.

Main Menu (Select One)

- Create a light source that sends signals.
- Design a telephone made from a paper cup and string.
- Create a pattern of drum beats.

Figure 4.17 The children each choose one option to complete and use the menu to assess their own progress, while the teacher assesses whether they met the appropriate standard.

Reducing Stress by Allowing Choice

Many children experience stress both in and outside of the classroom environment. You can find ways to alleviate stress within the classroom and school by creating an environment that is child-centered and focused on the interests of your students. In Chapter 2, we discussed the importance of creating a trauma-sensitive classroom, and in this chapter, we focus on how allowing choice can alleviate stress in some learners. Thompson and Breymen (2015) believed "students who are given choice in the classroom are more persistent and exhibit self-regulated learning behaviors" (p. 110).

In the Educator Standards, teachers are called to be collaborators who "demonstrate cultural competency when communicating with students, parents and colleagues and interact with them as co-collaborators in student learning" (ISTE, 2017). With this in mind, it's important for adults working with young children to be aware of families and the stresses children may be experiencing within their families. Also, you need to be aware of differences as well as similarities that exist among families so that you can best serve all families. Family systems theory consists of the notion that anything that happens to one member of the family affects all members of the family (Couchenour & Chrisman, 2014). We suggest the following tips to help create an environment that values differences and choices related to children and their families:

- When hosting family events, invite a variety of family members (Couchenour & Chrisman, 2014). Instead of having mother, father, and grandparent days, have days that include family members, but allow the child to choose who attends the event.

- Find out as much as possible about cultural differences and the individual child and his or her family. Provide choice in assignments that will allow families to share about their cultures if desired and to choose how they will share. For example, choices could be to share a tradition by coming in and talking to the class about the family's culture or by bringing in food related to the culture. In the following Community Connections section, Dr. Roberson reiterates the importance of getting to know the families and the community in which you teach to help you become an effective and culturally responsive educator.

- Include books in your classroom that display different cultures and a variety of people and situations. When children need to complete assignments related to books they've read, encourage them to choose from these books about their own or someone else's culture in the classroom.

- Use storytelling as a choice for children if they would like to share their stories and have their voices heard. In the following Community Connections section, Dr. Roberson stresses the importance of storytelling and providing a voice, especially to marginalized groups. If children are not comfortable with storytelling, allow for choice in how they will share their stories. For example, they could share using a video, a presentation, or other method.

Providing a variety of options to families on ways they can become involved with school is an important factor to consider. Brenda shared how important family engagement is to connecting family, school, and community:

Community Connections

Black Academic Experience and Cultural Responsiveness

Deborah Roberson, EdD

My doctoral research was about segregation and the disintegration of a neighborhood, the neighborhood where I grew up. My research consisted of the lived experiences of myself and other African Americans from the same neighborhood. The research recorded the story of segregation and desegregation and what effects it had on the black academic experience.

Our community worked because the teachers, families, and the community were supportive of one another. Everyone knew everybody. The neighborhood was segregated due in part because of the era and social and economic limitations, such as housing. However, the nice part of being segregated was that our community was our extended family. If a neighbor saw you about to get in trouble, they would go right to your family and they had permission to redirect you if needed. Regardless of your socioeconomic status, the black academic experience was threefold, it consisted of the school, the parents, and the community.

In my community when I was growing up, the teachers lived in the community. It was normal for the teachers to live in the community back then. There was always some kind of connection either through school, through church, or teachers having taught your parents. We were like a cocoon—all one thinking entity. When I had the opportunity to go to school with white children, my mom said to me after my first day in seventh grade (it was the first time I had a teacher who was white and had classmates who were white), "How was your day?" and I asked her why was she was asking me that. I didn't think one way or another, because kids are kids. We were never taught not to like someone because of their skin color. She was not sure how we would be treated and how I would react. When there was the choice for me to attend an elementary school with white children, my parents said no. They didn't want me or my siblings catching the bus into a white neighborhood; and they didn't want white teachers teaching us.

However, there is something to be said for a segregated community with limited resources. What makes it work is the meshing of the family, school, and the community, and the people living in the community that don't necessarily have children in the school but they

(continued on next page)

(continued from previous page)

know your family. I would tell teachers today it is all about building relationships with the family and that is not just by having a PTA meeting. You have to know the community. You have to be out there in the community. A lot of teachers do not live in the community where they work. When they leave school, they leave everything. I think it is important to be involved in the community, because when teachers are not a part of the community and do not know the fabric of the community, then they cannot understand the nuances that go on in that community. You have to understand the culture in which you work.

Teachers have a responsibility to get to know the children and learn about their cultures and to be inclusive. Just like we differentiate academics, we also need to differentiate to meet the needs of our students' cultures. There are things we can learn from different cultures. Respect where the children come from, what they do, how they do it, and then you can teach them effectively.

My research was guided by Critical Race Theory, which is based on race and racism. It is important to remember there is always a person/group that is dominant and a person/group that is marginalized. Because it is this way all the time does not mean it is the right way. Storytelling is an important tenet of Critical Race Theory as it gives marginalized groups the choice to share their lived experiences without prejudice. It is good to hear the stories of the children you teach. Even though they are little, little children will tell it all. Listening to people's stories gives you a window into who they are. Race and/or racism is something you live with if you are not from the dominant culture. But no one can take away your experiences or your truth. It is your truth. You can tell me the way most of the world thinks, but you can't tell me about my story because mine is not going to change to fit yours. It is important no matter whose culture it is, that their truths are voiced so others can hear their experiences.

From a personal perspective as a mom and a preschool teacher, I have seen first-hand the importance of family engagement for everyone—for kids, families, teachers, the districts, and the communities. Being a homeroom mom for my daughters has made them more enthusiastic about school, and their teachers are always so appreciative to have family members there to help out and show their support during class parties, field trips, visiting the classroom to read, and so on.

Helpful Tools for Assessing Creativity

We found the following resources helpful regarding assessing creativity, and we also developed our own rubric (Table 4.1) aligned with the ISTE Standards for Students to help us ensure children are exposed to well-rounded technology integration and that teachers are reflecting on the important components of the standards. This Creativity and Innovation Rubric can be used by students to self-assess the choices they have made within the classroom. After completing the self-assessment, the teacher and the student can discuss what they could do differently the next time or what they think they did well this time.

- Buck Institute for Education's list of rubrics for assessing creativity (www.bie.org/objects/cat/rubrics)
- Buck Institute for Education's K–2 Creativity and Innovation Rubric for PBL (www.bie.org/object/document/k_2_creativity_innovation_rubric)

Table 4.1 Creativity and Innovation Rubric—Aligned with ISTE Standards for Students

Empowered Learner

I take an active role in choosing technology and know how to use technology to demonstrate my learning.

Still Learning	Sometimes	Almost Always

Digital Citizen

I demonstrate responsibility and can identify strategies to keep me safe online.

Still Learning	Sometimes	Almost Always

(continued on next page)

Knowledge Constructor

I use technology to create and demonstrate learning and explore real-life problems.

Still Learning	Sometimes	Almost Always

Innovative Designer

I use technology to design, create, and innovate.

Still Learning	Sometimes	Almost Always

Computational Thinker

I use technology to solve problems and represent my thinking.

Still Learning	Sometimes	Almost Always

Creative Communicator

I communicate effectively when using technology and choose appropriate technology to help me communicate.

Still Learning	Sometimes	Almost Always

Global Collaborator

I use digital tools that help me to learn more about other people and cultures and work collaboratively with others.

Still Learning	Sometimes	Almost Always

This rubric can be found on our wiki (nurturingyounginnovators.wikispaces.com/Resources).

Project to Support Choice and Family Involvement

Math Family Night

This project was created for Grade 3 but can be modified for any grade.
Created by Meghan Czapka, Nicole Fantom, and Gabrielle Poole

Common Core State Standards addressed:

- CCSS.Math.Content.3.OA.A.1: Represent and solve problems involving multiplication and division.
- CCSS.Math.Content.3.NF.A.1: Develop understanding of fractions as numbers.

If Doing This...   Why Not Try This?

Filling Someone's Bucket.

The children all have their own buckets and they draw pictures or write kind things to their classmates to fill their buckets. This activity helps to build community in the classroom and self-esteem. Check out the Bucket Fillers website for more information (goo.gl/yD4u3g).

Create a Jar of Awesome.

Have each child decorate his or her own "jar of awesome." Whenever students accomplish something or reach a goal, have them complete a slip of paper and place it in their jars. Then, if children need to be reminded of their accomplishments or they are having a difficult day, they can go back to their jars of awesome and remind themselves of how awesome they are. This will also help to encourage a growth mindset and resilience. Find more information on the Shake Up Learning website (shakeuplearning.com/blog/jar-of-awesome).

Project-Based Learning:

The class is working on researching a science topic of interest to them that is related, in particular, to insects. Each child researches a specific insect and chooses how they will present their findings.

Create a Wonder Wall.

In order to help young children think about their passions and what they want to explore during genius hour, you can start with creating a Wonder Wall. On the Wonder Wall, list each child's name, and under each name, place sticky notes of things the child wonders about and is curious to learn more about (Letter, 2016). Common Sense Media provides a visual representation of this and more information on their blog (goo.gl/iaxfPp).

Family Tree Bulletin Board:

Families send in pictures to add to the family tree bulletin board. This is a great way to build community in the classroom.

Create a Family Slideshow Using a Digital Tool of Choice:

Students and families create a family digital slideshow that they present to or share with the school community. The slideshow's goals are for families to identify and define the characteristics of a family, to foster an understanding of the many types of family structure, and to explore their own family structure and the importance of their family to them. One of the authors made an example of a family video using PowerPoint (tinyurl.com/NYI-familyslideshow).

Ask students and their families to consider questions such as these:

- How do you decide what makes a family?
- In what ways are families unique?
- What is the importance of family to your life?

Estimated audience: (40 people; our class and families)

Theme: Carnival

Duration: 2 hours (6 p.m. to 8 p.m.)

Students have the choice to plan and create carnival activities they design with materials such as cardboard, open-ended materials, and so on.

When students and families enter, they will have their picture taken in the carnival booth. They can then walk freely around the gym to the activities the students are running.

The children can choose from the following activities:

- Balloon Darts: A dart is thrown at one balloon and a number will appear. Then a dart is thrown at another balloon and another number will appear. Using those two numbers, they will add, multiply and subtract
- Multiplication Hopscotch: Each square has a multiplication problem. When a player steps on a square, he or she has to answer the problem before moving on to the next step. This activity can be modified to use with addition or subtraction, depending on the age and ability of those taking part in the activity.
- Bottle Cap Fractions: A board has a series of addition fraction problems. Every bottle cap has a fraction that's a possible answer to the problem. After adding each fraction, players screw the bottle cap on.
- Higher or Lower: Cards are displayed on a board. Students go up to the board, choose two cards to compare, and then determine which card has the higher number and which has the lower.
- Guessing Game: There are two jars containing different numbers of objects. Students take a piece of paper and create a greater than/less than sentence for their guesses (e.g., 80 goldfish > 50 peanut butter cups)

At the end of each game, the students will give out the tickets to the winners. The tickets can be cashed in for a prize or put in a basket for a raffle.

- Multiplication Bingo (Conclusion Activity): Everyone plays! Each person is given a card with multiplication problems and products. The caller says the product and the multiplication problem. Prizes will be given to those who get bingo.

This "Family Math Night–Carnival Themed" Pinterest board (goo.gl/2J9ikU) has ideas on implementing this family math night.

+ Reflection Questions

Here are some questions to consider after you've completed this chapter:

- How do you provide choice to children?
- What kind of choices do you provide to children?
- How do children benefit when they are provided with choices?
- How do you encourage children to be creative communicators?
- How do you get to know the individual young learners you are working with?
- How can you provide choice that is related to family events to ensure you are inclusive of all families?
- What kind of digital tools/resources do you use? How do you, or could you, encourage young learners to use tools that personalize their learning?
- If you have tried genius hour, digital inquiry, and transformative learning techniques, what has been your experience? If you have not tried these strategies, how do you think they support individual children? What would you need in order to try these out if you have not done so yet?
- The Office of Educational Technology encourages adults to teach children how to have a growth mindset. In what ways do you do this, or will you do this, with the young learners you are working with?
- What kind of resources/support do you need for teaching young learners to have a growth mindset?

Makerspaces and Innovation Labs in the Classroom, Home, and Community

"What keeps life fascinating is the constant creativity of the soul."

—*Deepak Chopra*

This chapter provides practical examples and ideas on how early childhood educators can work with the community and families to create makerspaces in the three environments where young children spend the most time: school, home, and the community. The topic of this chapter aligns with the ISTE Standards for Educators as educators should serve as facilitators who "manage the use of technology and student learning strategies in digital platforms, virtual environments, hands-on makerspaces or in the field" (International Society for Technology in Education [ISTE], 2017). Within this chapter, we also revisit the importance of ensuring that learners are given opportunities to be innovative designers and computational thinkers.

Chapter Overview

This chapter will cover the following:

- The Maker Movement and making, creating, and inventing in the classroom, home, and community
- How to create a makerspace in both the classroom and the home
- Integrating technology and engineering skills within a makerspace
- Reflection questions related to encouraging making and creating

Student as Innovative Designer and Computational Thinker

"Students use a variety of technologies within a design process to identify and solve problems by creating new, useful or imaginative solutions."

— ISTE Standards for Students, Standard 4: Innovative Designer

"Students develop and employ strategies for understanding and solving problems in ways that leverage the power of technological methods to develop and test solutions."

— ISTE Standards for Students, Standard 5: Computational Thinker

Makerspaces provide an ideal environment to encourage young children to be innovative designers and computational thinkers. Making and inventing with open-ended materials help children learn how to generate ideas and problem solve, opening the door to creative thinking and design. In addition, activities like robotics and coding, which can be part of a maker practice, provide the computational thinking practice young learners need, allowing students to use technology and learn by trial and error. These activities teach young learners about algorithmic thinking and how to design and problem solve while analyzing data and steps in the design process.

In this chapter, we explore these topics and more, as we take a look at how to encourage making and innovation.

The Maker Movement—Turning Knowledge Into Action

Today, makerspaces are emerging in schools and libraries everywhere, and as Heraper (2017) stated, "Educational Makerspaces have the potential to revolutionize the way we approach teaching and learning. The Maker Movement is about moving from consumption to creation and turning knowledge into action" (p. 3).

The Maker Movement encourages children to think creatively, work creatively with others, and implement innovations. The goal of a makerspace is to provide tools, materials, and technology so that children can explore and be makers—spurred by their own imaginations and ideas. Thus, making in the classroom is an effective way to teach hands-on learning, inspiring children to be creators and not just consumers. Makerspaces integrate different subjects and expose children to critical content areas such as science, technology, engineering, the arts, and math (STEAM). Jarrett (2016) described the mission of the makerspace: to "help our learners become 'Life Ready,' developing a mindset defined by the qualities of caring, thinking, designing, and acting" (p. 51). In addition, students can gain skills such as empathy, collaboration, communication, creativity, and critical thinking—skills that are essential for surviving and thriving in a global society.

Because many of the creations in a makerspace can be shared outside of the school setting with the use of technology, makerspaces can help to redefine learning. The Maker Ed website (makered.org) offers many ideas for student creations in their Resource Library. These projects—such as a bike light, cupcake oven, and cloud lamp—demonstrate how a makerspace inspires creative thinking and how the creations can be showcased and shared with a broad audience. As each makerspace can include a variety of different materials, integrating a makerspace into

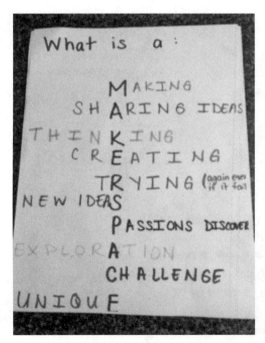

Figure 5.1 One activity you could have students do is draw a picture or complete an acrostic poem of what a makerspace is to them. Photo credit: Gail Switzer

Figure 5.2 Start out small with a bookshelf for your makerspace.

the classroom can be done on a limited budget, and no two makerspaces will look exactly the same (Figure 5.1).

Some makerspaces are housed within libraries or within an area of a classroom. But they need not be extensive at all; your makerspace could simply consist of a bin where you store a variety of materials for making or even one shelf on a bookshelf (Figure 5.2). Teachers can come together to develop a makerspace area for students, or part of a collaborative project can involve students and teachers creating the makerspace itself. Makerspaces can be tailored to the individual needs and interests of the students in your school, and the types of projects created within one are infinite.

Peg shared the following about using makerspaces in her classroom:

> I have a makerspace in my classroom that the children work coopera-
> tively with. They think of an idea, plan it out, create it, and after testing it,
> they try to make their idea better. I add different materials and take some
> away after I see them using them a lot. This helps them stay creative
> in their design process. In addition, we use a Makey Makey to explore
> coding and creativity!

Start Small

If you haven't started making yet, here are some suggestions to get started:

- Begin small and don't be afraid to make mistakes. Any time we start something new, we are taking a risk. Risks are all part of the making experience and we want to model to our students that risk-taking and making mistakes is all part of the process.
- Create STEAM bins and add items to the bins that would encourage building, making, and creating. For example, one STEAM bin might include toothpicks and playdough. Children can be provided task cards with both pictures and words (a boat, a house, etc.) to choose from.
- Use tinker trays/boxes to encourage making and creating in your classroom. Meri Cherry provides an example on her website (goo.gl/WQhf9u).
- Search for ideas on how to implement a makerspace. The Pinterest board "Makerspace in Early Childhood" (goo.gl/DSUkwJ) has many practical ideas for how to do this on a limited budget.
- Buy inexpensive items to add to your makerspace.

Use recycled materials to encourage making, and ask families to donate materials to the classroom.

Here is a sample list of inexpensive items you could purchase (or find used/recycled) to help you get started making. We've also included a wish list of items that are more expensive.

Sample Shopping List to Get Started on Making: Inexpensive Items

- Toolbox
- Hammer
- Wire cutters
- Soldering gun kit (adult use only)
- Wire
- Cell batteries
- Saw
- Screwdrivers
- Nails
- K'NEX Education: Kid K'NEX Group Set (for ages 3 and up)
- Safety goggles
- Glue gun (adult use only)
- Beads
- Fasteners
- Pegboards
- Buttons
- Cups
- Empty paper towel rolls
- Toilet paper rolls
- Egg cartons
- Straws
- Q-tips (or cotton swabs)_
- Coffee filters
- Popsicle sticks

Sample Wish List: More Expensive Items

- Makey Makey Classic (goo.gl/wSDNfP): This is an invention kit for everyone that encourages art, engineering, and imagination.
- littleBits STEAM Student Set (littlebits.cc/kits/steam-student-set): These kits provide hands-on STEAM activities and challenges for students to design and create.
- Hummingbird Robotics Kit from BirdBrain Technologies (tinyurl.com/NYI-hummingbird): This classroom kit for 8 to 12 students provides electronics and materials needed to build robots.
- Compact 3D printer: A 3D printer provides a way for students to design and create 3D projects. There are many 3D printers on the market; an example of a compact 3D printer is the CoLiDo Compact (goo.gl/2YCYbt).
- LEGO Education: Sets available from LEGO Education (education.lego.com) provide students with opportunities to design and code their designs.

Makerspaces and STEAM

According to Maslyk (2016), "STEAM and making are strategies that make sense for different types of learners. Personalization makes that possible. The hands-on nature of this work lends itself to true student learning" (pp. 13–14). Personalization is a common theme discussed regarding nurturing young innovators, and makerspaces and STEAM allow learners to explore their different interests. Makerspaces and STEAM also cater to students who prefer hands-on learning.

Makerspaces are built on the constructivist theory, and in a makerspace and in many of the STEAM activities we discuss in this chapter, students are making, creating, and innovating while learning. When we talk about makerspaces and STEAM, we are thinking of them as places for young learners to make, create, and innovate with topics that many times integrate science, technology, engineering, the arts, and math. Rendina (2015) stated that "educators have discovered the power of makerspaces in schools to build students' competencies and interest in science, technology, engineering and math" (para. 1). The acronym STEM stands for science, technology, engineering, and math, but in STEAM, the "A" has been added for "the arts," which is one reason why STEAM activities are a good addition to makerspace environments that encourage creativity and innovation. Young children especially learn through their experiences, and making is an ideal way to foster their natural creative abilities as well as to find creative ways to integrate STEAM activities like coding, robotics, and design thinking.

We created STEAM bins so that children could be interactive and make with materials and task cards. We purchased hard pencil boxes from the dollar store and labeled each box with pictures and names of the items in the box. You can purchase or find free templates for your bins at TeachersPayTeachers (teacherspayteachers.com), or you can create the templates yourself. The ideas for bins are endless, but the main point is to have each bin contain items that children can explore, think about, and create with. Here are some ideas for what to include in STEAM bins.

Ideas for STEAM Bins

- Bin 1: Straws, deck of cards, and tape
- Bin 2: Aluminum foil and pencils
- Bin 3: Toothpicks and playdough
- Bin 4: Buttons and playdough
- Bin 5: Plastic cups and Popsicle sticks

- Bin 6: Cardboard and PVC pipe (may need a bigger container for these pieces)
- Bin 7: Plastic eggs, plastic spoons, and rubber bands
- Bin 8: Empty toilet paper rolls and duct tape

In each bin, you can provide pictures/task cards for children to choose from for ideas of things to build and create. For younger children, you can use pictures only to give them the choices. For older children, you can create specific tasks that you ask them to choose from. Figures 5.3 and 5.4 show examples of task cards for different age levels. For a younger child, you can provide multiple task cards with pictures to choose from.

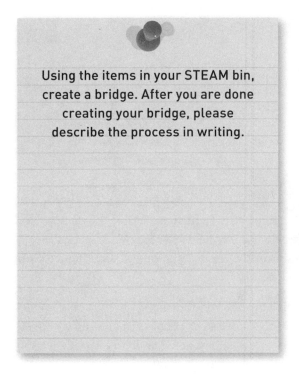

Figure 5.3 A sample STEAM task card used for children who can read. The items in the STEAM bin will vary, and this activity promotes engineering and design thinking, while the writing piece integrates language arts.

Figure 5.4 A sample picture task card for STEAM bins. A picture task card can help prompt young learners as they explore the materials in the bins. It still allows for creativity because children use a variety of tools to re-create the image. Photo credit: Tracey Woodruff Brown

Developing Soft Skills in Makerspaces

Makerspaces provide a multitude of opportunities for young children to develop soft skills such as resilience, collaboration, problem solving, creativity, and perserverance. Lacey (2017) stated "collaboration, problem-solving, real world learning, the value of failure, perseverance and creativity enable students to interact effectively and harmoniously with other people" (p. 23). When young innovators are provided with the space to create, make, and invent, this naturally promotes the 4Cs (communication, critical thinking, collaboration, and creativity), which are also soft skills but critical digital age skills. These student-led activities taking place within a makerspace environment are academic as well as social, which is also a soft skill. Lynch (2017) provided the following insight related to how makerspaces focus on creating and social skills:

> In Makerspaces students are given opportunities to work with technology, bring ideas to life, interact with peers and educators in new ways, and learn to problem solve, as well as, providing an environment in which they can make mistakes and learn from them. With all of the opportunities for learning that they offer, makerspaces may hold the key to unlocking the potential for innovation in our students and our economy. (para. 8)

Adults working with young children act as facilitators, setting up the environment, and asking productive questions during and after making. Children should be encouraged to use all the resources they have at their disposal, including their peers, technology, and their families.

Apodaca (2017) suggested the following: "To build autonomy, give your makers the freedom to not only choose the projects they work on, but also how they work on them. Makerspaces flourish when their members are allowed to tinker with independent projects" (p. 7). Makerspaces provide an excellent opportunity for students to practice the soft skills of problem solving (when making decisions on what to make), collaborating (when working with others during making), and communicating (when showcasing what they made, created, and invented with others).

Peg shared the following tip for facilitating learning and encouraging soft skills such as being a self-directed learner and resilient when making:

Stop trying to have children conform to you. Let them learn what they want to learn, how they want to learn, when they want to learn it, and where they want to learn it. You can guide them and facilitate their learning. Let them feel that they are "tiny teachers" and they are responsible for their learning and the learning of others in their class. Your room may be loud and messy, but the learning is just as obvious!

Makerspaces in the Home

Families can also create inexpensive makerspaces in their homes to encourage their children to continue discovering and creating outside of school (Figure 5.5). A makerspace in the home can be on a smaller scale and does not need as many materials as a makerspace in the school. Many items that can be used to create a home makerspace are commonly found in the home.

Figure 5.5 Example of how families can create a makerspace at home. The young children (Kingston, age 8, and Kennedy, age 5) are engaged in this home makerspace. Photo credit: Stephanie Budhai

Community Connections

Father and Daughter Innovation Time

Michael and Marlee Porter

Michael shared an activity that he and his daughter, Marlee, did at home. They decided to gather materials and create a catapult (Figure 5.6). The materials used to make a catapult can vary; you can make a miniature catapult with Popsicle sticks and other household items. Michael and Marlee used real wood pieces to re-create Leonardo da Vinci's 15th century catapult. Michael shared the following information regarding his creation: "Catapults were first invented in ancient Greek and Roman times, however our common idea of them is based on drawings we have from the Medieval Ages. Leonardo redesigned the catapult around 1485, and used the spring-like energy stored in bent wood to give power to the swing arm."

For other ideas on how to make catapults at home or in the classroom, please check Kids Activities Blog (goo.gl/cw4bE7).

Figure 5.6 Michael and Marlee Porter enjoy making together as father and daughter, and they re-created a catapult for this project. This is an excellent way to encourage STEAM activities in young children.

Commonly Used Items Found in Homes for Making

- Cardboard boxes: shoebox, cereal box, packing box
- Paper: envelopes from postal mail, flyers, and store advertisements
- Batteries
- Wine corks
- Soda cans
- Water bottles
- Bottle caps or jar lids
- Spoons
- Fabric scraps
- Office supplies: tape, scissors, staplers, paper cutter, index cards, glue gun

Integrating Technology and Engineering

Within a makerspace environment, young learners need opportunities to explore science, technology, engineering, the arts, and math. Robotics and coding are important digital age skills to expose young learners to early on. We have seen the excitement and engagement that occurs when children see their robots move or the computer avatars they coded become animated on a screen.

Robotics

Including materials in the classroom for young children to explore robotics is a fascinating and fun process and a good addition to making in the classroom. Sullivan and Bers (2015) conducted a study integrating robotics for eight weeks with students in prekindergarten through second grade. Research supported the idea that the use of robotics as well as coding provides "early childhood teachers a new and exciting way to address the 'T' of technology and 'E' of engineering that are most neglected in early childhood STEM education" (Sullivan & Bers, 2015, p. 16). It is a good idea to provide a variety of materials and have children explore and work in groups to come up with a plan to create their robot. The internet is a good source of information and children can either look for information themselves or they can be assisted by an adult. For example, on the Instructables website (instructables.com/id/Make-a-Vibrobot), you can find a video and instructions for how to make a vibrating robot.

Materials you will need:

- Vibrating motor with wires
- Cell battery

- Toothbrush
- Something to affix the battery to the toothbrush (we used two-sided tape)

During activities like this, young children will learn how to problem solve, how to collaborate with others, and how to think critically. This activity is a hands-on, trial-and-error type of activity.

In Laura's science methods course, which covers PK to fourth-grade science teaching, her students explored making and creating and inventing each week. The class was also planning a family and community makerspace event in which they would showcase what they had been doing in their science methods class and then provide opportunities for their families and the community to make, create, and invent with them. During one of the classes, the students were provided materials they could use to make a small vibrating robot. After making the motor, the students researched how to make other robots and ultimately, they found an Instructables video that illustrates the process of making a Solo Cup Art Robot (www.instructables.com/id/Solo-Cup-Artbot). They worked on their robot until they got it functioning (Figure 5.7); then they named the robot and put it on display for everyone to see. The whole class collaborated in making this one robot and were

Figure 5.7 Students created an art bot from recycled and household materials. The students were proud of their accomplishment.

Figure 5.8 At the Family and Community Makerspace Night, a student makes a robot with the materials provided.

excited with their success. We later hosted our family and community makerspace night in which children and families could make robots, make, and create together (Figure 5.8).

Coding

Increasingly, the ability to code has become an important skill to introduce to young children. Yongpradit (2017) stated that "computer science is not just an opportunity for developing 21st century skills such as creativity and problem solving, it is also a fundamental 21st century subject, on the same level as language arts, mathematics, and science" (para. 6). If you want young children to be prepared for a technology-driven and media-rich society, you must provide them as many chances as possible to develop these skills.

Coding skills can be developed without technology, and Code.org (https://code.org/curriculum/unplugged) provides a list of non-technology-based activities that you can do to help children learn the basics. An example lesson has one child acting as the coder and another child as a robot, with the coder instructing the robot to perform specific actions. This kinesthetic activity can support young learners in

Figure 5.9 Coding is an excellent way to integrate the T (technology) and E (engineering) of STEAM as young children develop design skills.

Figure 5.10 Families, students, and teachers talk about coding at Family and Community Makerspace Night. Coding integrates technology and design thinking, which are digital age skills children need to learn.

grasping a fundamental part of coding. We also included coding at our family and community makerspace event and children and families had opportunities to code together (Figures 5.9 and 5.10).

Here are some great resources to check out to learn more about how to teach coding to young learners:

- Code.org (https://code.org) provides excellent resources to get anyone started with coding. You could do an Hour of Code and receive a free certificate, which can be a motivator to code again.
- ScratchJr (https://scratchjr.org) is a tool children ages 5 to 7 can use to learn how to code and create interactive games and stories.
- Mitch Resnick's TED Talk "Let's Teach Kids to Code" (goo.gl/OsVSVO) provides good information about the benefits of teaching kids to code.
- Tynker (https://www.tynker.com) is a learning system that teaches children ages 7 and up to be makers and creators through creating apps, building games, and exploring STEM activities.
- In his post on Edutopia (goo.gl/Hy0luC), Matt Davis provides resources to help parents teach their kids to code.

Projects to Inspire Making, Innovating, and Family and Community Involvement

Here are some projects to encourage families and the community to participate in the making process.

Cardboard Challenge Event

This project can be used with any grade level.

Provide students with cardboard boxes of all different sizes, as well as materials like glue, scissors, construction paper, duct tape, and straws. Ask students to use their creativity to create something collaboratively together. Whatever they create should have a purpose. For example, if you are studying a particular content area, such as geometry, you could have young learners create something using shapes and then have them explain what they created and the shapes that they used. Figures 5.11 through 5.13 show creations that resulted when students were given open-ended materials and boxes. The only requirement that students were given was that whatever they made had to relate back to math. The groups re-created a

If Doing This... Why Not Try This?

STEAM Bins: If providing children opportunities to work with STEAM challenges in the classroom

Create STEAM Challenge Games: Give children STEAM challenges to complete at home with their family as part of a take-home activity. The Playtivities blog (playtivities.com/stem-challenges-family) offers multiple ideas.

Making in the Classroom

Set up a Badging System: Set up a badging system and explain to students what they need to do to obtain a badge. Badges provide validation that they have accomplished a goal that they set. Badges can also be physical or digital.

Encouraging an Environment That Values Mistakes and Risk-Raking

Implement a Failures Box. Have children document their making experiences by drawing pictures and writing (if appropriate) about them. In the book *Meaningful Making: Projects and Inspirations for Fab Labs and Makerspaces* (goo.gl/UoEvqL), Susanna Tesconi (2016) provides more information on using a "failures box" to help children build shared knowledge and practice telling their stories.

Figure 5.11 Students re-created a Sims house during the Cardboard Challenge. This allowed them to create a game they enjoyed playing outside of school, and they were able to use their imagination to create their Sims house out of cardboard.

Figure 5.12 Students created a Planko game out of cardboard and other materials. The Cardboard Challenge encouraged students to use their creativity while creating something that related to math.

Figure 5.13 Students created a Lucky Pot O' Gold game out of cardboard during the Cardboard Challenge.

Sims home (Figure 5.11), a Planko game (Figure 5.12), and a Lucky Pot O' Gold game (Figure 5.13).

On the Imagination Foundation website (cardboard-challenge.com/about) you can find out more about the Global Cardboard Challenge and how a boy named Caine inspired it by creating an arcade out of cardboard.

Family and Friends Makerspace Event—Come Make with Us!

This project can be used with any grade level.

After providing students with several opportunities to make, create, and invent during the school year, a final activity that you can hold is a Family and Friends Makerspace Event. This can be a class event or a school-wide event if other teachers would like to collaborate. Getting permission early for the event and deciding on the date, time, and who will be included are important first steps.

For this project, assign students to work in groups of approximately three to four peers. Have each group decide on a focus—the students will be the ones to plan and implement the activities for the Makerspace Event. Each group should have a different theme, but all themes need to relate back to making and creating. Depending on students' grade level, this list of responsibilities can be modified.

Have students create a poster presentation that is creative and includes the following items: pictures/graphics, information on their topic, a list of helpful resources/websites to find more information on the topic, and a page on the class wiki or website that can be shared with the community.

Students should expect to spend the following amount of time on their project:

- 2 to 3 hours of collaborative research, which includes brainstorming, looking for information, organizing information, and determining a layout/use of the space
- 2 hours of printing, crafting, and creating the actual content
- 2 hours putting together an online resource on the class wiki or website
- 2 hours of time to showcase their work at the event and to make with families and friends

Have each group choose a different topic. Here are some ideas:

- Coding
- Robotics—making robots from parts
- Recycle and Reuse—using recycled items to create, make, and invent
- Adding the A (the Arts) to STEM Centers to Create STEAM Centers

Be sure to send out invitations prior to the event (Figure 5.14). The event should be an opportunity to showcase student work and provide friends and families opportunities to explore making, creating, and inventing.

Family and Friends Makerspace Event

Come Create, Invent, and Learn with Us!

Date   Time   Location

The students and teachers at _____ are hosting a makerspace event on _____ from _____ to _____ in the _____. The students will share ideas on why makerspaces are important and how they can be used to teach critical 21st century skills. Makerspaces bring people together and allow for hands-on exploration focused on creating, inventing, and learning. Please stop by and take part in our making event. We will have light refreshments and the group topics include:

- Coding
- Robotics—making robots from parts
- Recycle and Reuse—using recycled items to create, make, and invent
- Adding the A (the Arts) to STEM Centers to Create STEAM Centers

We hope to see you and look forward to making, creating and inventing with you!

Figure 5.14 Sample invitation for a Family and Friends Makerspace Event.

Fairy Tale Engineering

This project was submitted by the Discovery teachers of the Wilson School District in West Lawn, Pennsylvania, who work with all students throughout the district as part of an elementary STEAM special. The Discovery special lasts for forty minutes, and students meet in the Discovery Lab once every six days. During this time, Discovery teachers introduce the youngest innovators in the district to simple machines through fairy tales. Fairy tale engineering introduces students to a basic design process framework and helps them connect this learning to fairy tales.

Students in kindergarten and first grade students use simple machines to help well-known fairy tale characters navigate their stories in a new way. Students are given a task that ignites their creativity and challenges them to design a solution to help the fairy tale characters. These young innovators use their knowledge of levers to create catapults for Little Red Riding Hood to deliver cookies to Grandma's house (Figure 5.15). Their imaginations help them create a car for the Three Billy Goats Gruff to safely travel across the evil troll bridge. Students use their prior knowledge and experiences to help the Gingerbread Man build a boat to cross the river, and they work collaboratively to make a ladder that helps Rapunzel escape safely from the evil witch. All of these activities are created using upcycled materials and amazing creativity from the students. These unique learning experiences give the young students at Wilson a hands-on approach to learning and failure. The

Figure 5.15 Students used upcycled materials to re-create the story of Little Red Riding Hood. After exploring simple machines, they created catapults to help Little Red Riding Hood deliver cookies to Grandma's house. Photo credit: Michael Creed

cross-curricular experience also helps these young innovators to develop skills such as the 4Cs—communication, collaboration, critical thinking, and creativity— which will be evident beyond their educational journey through Discovery.

+ Reflection Questions

Here are some questions to consider after you've completed this chapter:

- In order to create a path for creativity for young innovators, what might you want to modify or add to your classroom or school?
- What kind of materials do you or can you add that will provoke children to think critically and creatively?
- How can you or how do you create a culture of adventure and fun and wonder in your classroom?
- What kind of interests do the young children you are working with have? How can you use these interests to plan activities?
- What kind of resources do you currently have that would support a makerspace environment?
- How can you or do you collaborate with colleagues to support making?
- What kind of support do you have toward making with young children?
- How can you or do you involve families with making with children?
- What one thing will you try after reading this chapter?

Preparing Young Learners Through Community-Based Activities

"Education is for improving the lives of others and for leaving your community and world better than you found it."

—*Marian Wright Edelman*

This chapter focuses on ways to leverage media and technology to carry out impactful service-learning and project-based learning activities that are relevant to the lives of young children. We discuss how to engage families and the community with ideas that can be implemented within your own communities. In addition, we address how teachers can "create experiences for learners to make positive, socially responsible contributions and exhibit empathetic behavior online that builds relationships and community" (International Society for Technology in Education [ISTE], Standards for Educators, 2017).

Chapter Overview

This chapter will cover the following:

- Providing students with opportunities to be global collaborators
- Engaging students in experiential learning, such as service-learning and project-based learning
- Supporting civic engagement in students' learning, including activities such as play and role play

- Projects that connect families, communities, and students and that share ideas responsibly with the broader community
- Reflection questions related to preparing young learners and facilitating community-based learning activities

Student as Global Collaborator

"Students use digital tools to broaden their perspectives and enrich their learning by collaborating with others and working effectively in teams locally and globally."

— *ISTE Standards for Students, Standard 7: Global Collaborator*

Community-based projects provide opportunities for young learners to develop as global collaborators. Students broaden their persepectives through connecting with others from a variety of backgrounds and cultures. Being global citizens involves participating in robust projects that involve using collaborative tools and technologies to work with others to investigate problems and generate solutions. Here, we discuss some of the ways to bring creativity and innovation to community involvement through experiential learning and civic engagement.

Adults can model for young children how to positively and responsibly connect with families and the broader community online through social media. In this chapter, we share specific service-learning examples that provide ways to engage families and the community through social media and other tools.

Experiential Education

According to the Association for Experiential Education (n.d.), experiential education is "a philosophy that informs many methodologies in which educators purposefully engage with learners in direct experience and focused reflection in order to increase knowledge, develop skills, clarify values, and develop people's capacity to contribute to their communities" (para 2). When students are involved in experiential learning, they are required to go beyond classroom walls and learn in real-world contexts. Facing real-life issues and situations can encourage students to think creatively and innovatively. The Melbourne Child Psychology practice (2017) provided the following explanation of how experiential learning inspires creativity:

Experiential learning is collaborative and enables children to work out their own unique strategy (with some support), rather than following a set formula to arrive at an answer. They will be more likely to think creatively in the future, rather than assuming that all problems have "right" and "wrong" answers and "right" and "wrong" ways of getting there. (para. 8)

Service-Learning

Most are familiar with the concept of community service, in which individuals volunteer their time to support a human services mission. Service-learning is a pedagogical technique that combines engaging in community service with a clear purpose to connect the service experience with content learned in school. Mandy shared multiple ways her school for prekindergarten through fifth grade integrates service-learning:

- We hold a sock hop dance party with a DJ, photo booth, and dodgeball games. Everyone attending gives a donation of any amount, and it goes to our "sister" school, the Brain Tree School in Uganda.
- A lot of the kids also voluntarily do a "no gifts" birthday party and ask that a donation be made to either the Children's Hospital of Philadelphia or the Brain Tree School. We've been to two parties this year where the students requested donations instead of gifts.
- We just did a food drive two weeks ago, and a month before that, we did our annual coat drive, in which we donated clothes to an underprivileged school in Philadelphia.
- On MLK Day we are off, but the schools stay open for kids to make sandwiches and pack boxes of donated food, or some other kind of service.
- Every Thanksgiving we give food and money and feed over 2,000 needy families in Philadelphia. We spend a morning packing boxes of Thanksgiving meals, and everyone gets a turkey.

Critical reflection and making meaning of the service-learning experience are part of the service experience and act as mechanisms for students to think deeply about their civic commitment in relation to their course content. And often times, service-learning can help prepare students for their future professional careers. Jacoby (1999) defines service-learning as a "form of experiential education in which students engage in activities that address human and community needs together with structured opportunities intentionally designed to promote student learning and development" (p. 20). An important distinction between service-learning and community service is that the goal of service-learning is to use the experience of addressing community needs as an authentic lab connected to academic content.

Christiana and DeShawn created a service-learning project with the purpose of connecting with the community and helping students to learn different ways to keep their community clean and decorative while also applying their knowledge of geometrical shapes. Christiana and DeShawn connected their activity to Pennsylvania Core Mathematics Standard CC.2.3.4.A.1: Draw lines and angles and identify these in two-dimensional figures.

When asked how this service-learning project would integrate students, families, and communities, they responded with the following information:

- The children will create different geometrical shapes that will be included in their art projects for the parks, as well as help in the cleanup of the parks.
- All families will be asked to utilize their talents in the park cleanups. They will be asked to partake in the following: cleaning up the parks, decorating the parks, or donating supplies and/or monetary funds to the project.
- Community members will be asked to utilize their talents in the park cleanups. They will be asked to partake in the following: cleaning up the parks, decorating the parks, or donating supplies and/or monetary funds to the project. For example, some members may be contractors, architects, painters, recreational cleaners, or landscapers.

The organizers shared some ideas on how to publicize the event:

- Schools can advertise the event through social media (e.g., Facebook, Twitter, Instagram).
- A call to community members can go out through social media to invite anyone who is interested to participate and share their talents related to this community service project.
- During and after the event, photos and videos can be shared showcasing the results of the project. Note that photos of students should not be included on social media or any kind of documentation (letters, flyers, etc.) unless written permission is received beforehand. Also, always be aware of your district's policies related to sharing information.

Project-Based Learning

Project-based learning allows for students to tackle real-world problems based on their interests, working collaboratively. The outcomes and benefits of this type of learning have been identified by the Buck Institute for Education (2017), which has stated that project-based learning

- Makes school more engaging for students;
- Improves learning;
- Builds success skills for college, career, and life;
- Helps address standards;
- Provides opportunities for students to use technology;
- Makes technology more enjoyable and rewarding; and
- Connects students and schools with communities and the real world.

Cecily and Rene worked together to create a food drive in their school. This activity connected their students to the community and to the real world. The purpose of the activity was to "help provide food to families/people that go without or [who] may be unfortunate [and uable] to afford certain food items."

When asked how this project met state standards, Cecily and Rene spoke of the importance of teaching students about nutrition and the five food groups and how they play a key role in everyday life. In addition to helping students build character through community involvement, they stated that the project connected to the following standards:

- Pennsylvania Early Childhood Education Standard 10.1.2.C1: Students will be able to identify foods and the roles they have in keeping our bodies healthy.
- National Health Education Standard 4: Students will demonstrate the ability to use interpersonal communication skills to enhance health and avoid or reduce health risk.

Cecily and Rene provided the following ways they would use technology to advertise and share information about this event:

- Post on the school website details about the event and an invitation to involve community members and families.
- Post on Facebook ways families and the community can help support this event.

- Have teachers and children create a blog to promote the food drives. An example of a digital tool that is safe and easy to use is Kidblog (https://kidblog.org/home). Creating a blog with young children is a great opportunity to stress the importance of being a safe, responsible digital citizen when communicating online.

Civic Engagement

Community-based learning serves as an ideal opportunity for young learners to explore civic engagement. Children need experiences to learn how to be good citizens. Herczog (2016) stated:

> There is hardly a teacher, school administrator, parent or policymaker who will deny that every one of our students needs to understand and embrace their role as future citizens to ensure that our American democracy is sustained, strengthened and valued. (p. 24)

Because time is an issue for many teachers, it may be a challenge to fit civic engagement within the school day. There are many ways to integrate and support civic engagement in learning, such as service-learning projects, class discussions, role play, and home and school connections (Levin-Goldberg, 2009, p. 15). Service-learning projects, as previously described, can focus on civic engagement. In addition, young children can learn about civic engagement through play. NYU Steinhardt (2017) shared:

> Classroom-based play provides an opportunity for children to develop executive functions, including controlling emotions, resisting impulses, and exerting self-control. Through play, children learn to become a member of a social group and follow rules, foreshadowing the skills and behaviors of a civically engaged adolescent or adult. (para. 8)

Home and school connections provide an effective avenue for communicating with families about the importance of civic engagement, and involving families in projects will help create a culture where civic engagement is "sustained, strengthened, and valued" (Herczog, 2016, p. 24).

The Partnership for 21st Century Learning (P21) (2016) included civic literacy as part of its framework for essential skills students need in order to be successful in a global society. In fact, P21 (2016) has stated that "schools must move beyond a focus on basic competency to promoting understanding of academic content at much higher levels by weaving 21st century interdisciplinary themes" (p.2). Civic literacy is one of these interdisciplinary themes, and its learning outcomes are described as follows:

- Participating effectively in civic life through knowing how to stay informed and understanding governmental processes;
- Exercising the rights and obligations of citizenship at local, state, national, and global levels; and
- Understanding the local and global implications of civic decisions. (p. 2)

Tools for Experiential Learning Projects

A wide assortment of digital tools are available to help facilitate experiential learning projects. There are four components to focus on while facilitating these projects: communication, collaboration, reflection, and sharing/disseminating information. We'll break down the tools using those categories.

Communication

A large part of experiential learning projects involves communicating with others, including getting the word out to the community and families. We stress the importance of modeling to young children responsible and safe use of digital tools when communicating with others. It is important to intentionally discuss what you are modeling, so the children understand and can learn how to communicate in a safe and responsible way.

Here are some examples of communication tools that we recommend:

- For alternatives to phone calls or in-person communication, use social media (e.g., Facebook messaging, WhatsApp) and/or video conferencing (e.g., Appear.In, Talky, Google Hangouts, Apple Facetime, Zoom).
- For written feedback, use a tool such as Google Forms for creating invitations and opportunities to RSVP.

Collaboration

Experiential learning activities such as service-learning and project-based learning are not completed in isolation. Teams are typically formed, which calls for ways for students to make contributions and share ideas.

Here are some tools we recommend for collaboration:

- Google Drive (https://www.google.com/drive)
- Microsoft OneDrive (https://onedrive.live.com)
- Dropbox (https://www.dropbox.com)
- Amazon Drive (https://www.amazon.com/clouddrive)
- Apple iCloud (https://www.apple.com/icloud)

Reflection

Because a critical component of service-learning and project-based learning is reflecting on how things are going so that you can make adjustments as you go forward, it's important to provide students with a way to reflect on their learning experiences.

Here are some tools we recommend for such reflection:

- Vlogging: A vlog is a blog made with video. Tools for creating and editing video for vlogging include Vlogr (www.vlogr.it), PocketVideo (https://pocket.video), MixBit (https://mixbit.com/home), and Voice-Thread (https://voicethread.com).
- Podcast series: These are recorded sessions that focus on specific topics. Some tools for creating podcasts include Opinion (www.opinionpod casting.com), PodBean (www.podbean.com), Shoutem (www.shoutem .com/app/podcast), and ipadio (www.ipadio.com).

Dissemination

Once the service-learning or project-based learning experience has concluded, there are many ways to share final products with the larger community or world. As we discussed previously, it is always important to remember to obtain permission for sharing information or pictures of children with the larger community.

Here are some formats and tools we recommend for sharing final work:

- Digital portfolio: Easy Portfolio (thepegeekapps.com/portfolio), Seesaw (https://web.seesaw.me), and Google Sites (https://sites.google.com)
- Multimedia video: iMovie (https://www.apple.com/imovie), VidLab (https://museworks.co/vidlab), and Magisto (https://www.magisto.com)
- Interactive presentation: SlideDog (https://slidedog.com), Present.me (https://present.me/content), and Haiku Deck (www.haikudeck.com)

Community Connections

Service-Learning Projects

Quibila Divine, African American Family Services Agency, Community Member

I work with an organization called the Women's Christian Alliance, which is the oldest African-American family services agency in Philadelphia. I previously worked with a program called Youth Ready, and we provided students with a service-learning project. The first year, it was focused on homelessness; we had the students decide what programs they wanted to work on and how many activities they wanted to do. The students decided they wanted to feed the homeless and go to the downtown area to interview the homeless people. Additionally, they helped sell newspapers, and the proceeds went to the homeless. Because there were three different activities, the students broke into three groups and came back together to share their experiences and do a city-wide presentation about their experiences. The second year, the students focused on violence and crime prevention, the effects it had on the neighborhood, and what community members can do as individuals to reduce crime. The third year, students worked on public school budgets. They had a panel discussion with one of the school reform commissions, the city controller, and the superintendents of neighborhood networks. They also went to Harrisburg to engage in advocacy activities in the state.

For students, they were able to pick up on digital age skills from the standpoint of understanding the need to be flexible and choose with the team how to approach the project. They also learned how to be accountable. Students also constructed a creative poster that demonstrated a variety of skills that they learned. For community members, we had a town hall meeting and invited families and community members to come out, as well as the panel of community members, family members, and elected officials who were able to share their perspectives of the different areas being tackled.

The creativity came with the presentation, display board, and delivery of the content, and also the collaboration that took place to make the service experiences successful. Because many

(continued on next page)

(continued from previous page)

of the students came back year after year, we were able to see the progression and growth in their creativity. The way that the town hall meetings occurred was a creative way to educate others in the community about the topics they were working on.

The students were required to use technology to present their learning and master Microsoft Office Suite tools. Each student was flexible and used different tools; for example, some used video recording devices to capture the interview data. The students advertised and created flyers to invite the panelist and community members. Everyone had a voice in the collaborative community of learning.

You have to allow the families to put insight into working with their children, because they know their children the best. When dealing with the whole family, it is good to get them involved. Some of the families helped with making phone calls and securing the speakers and panelists. It is very important for us as adults to serve as positive role models for children. Sometimes children are looked at as not important; it is important to welcome diversity and to be flexible.

Peg described a variety of ways technology is used in her classroom to support digital citizenship and global collaboration:

> My classroom is a fully blended education classroom. Critical thinking is happening while the children are being independent learners using adaptive digital curriculum programs for math and language arts. We've used Office 365 to create service projects, create and participate in discussion boards, Skype one another, and work on shared documents. We have used SharePoint to communicate with students in Jordan. With the classroom in Jordan we shared and gave feedback to one another regarding our student authored books. We use OneNote for Classrooms to share materials and references students may need to access at home. I am currently developing a self-paced online math class for some of my students to work on. Using technology is just the culture in our room.

If Doing This... Why Not Try This? ›››››

Community Service

Service-Learning: Instead of choosing a nonprofit organization to volunteer at, develop a collaborative global service-learning experience for students in which the human services project they focus on is connected to their course content. For example, you can develop a service-learning project working with a school in another country. Have your students become language partners with students at an international school where they don't have an ELL teacher, but have the desire to learn the primary language of the students at the other school. The service-learning experience should be built on reciprocity, and all parties should benefit from the experience. Students would be building skills related to course content, such as writing and oral language skills, and also strengthening digital age skills, such as collaboration and communication.

Recycling Paper

Create a Community Recycling Initiative: Many classroom teachers recycle paper to use as scrap or for project materials. A variety of other items can also be recycled and used in projects. Think about creating a community recycling initiative that encourages families and community businesses to collect a different item each month that students can use for arts and innovation projects. You can create tracking charts to inspire healthy competition. Here are a few ideas for item themes:

- January: Toilet paper rolls
- February: Plastic containers (e.g., from restaurant leftovers)
- March: Paper
- April: Empty tape rolls
- May: Plastic cups
- June: Empty glue stick rolls
- July: Plastic bags
- August: Plastic utensils
- September: Empty aluminum foil and plastic wrap rolls
- October: Plastic bowls
- November: Expired batteries
- December: Paper towel rolls

(continued on next page)

(continued from previous page)

If Doing This...	Why Not Try This?
Discussing the Local Community	**Hold a Community Member Day:** Oftentimes, part of the curriculum involves discussing the local community and neighborhoods. In addition to learning about the surrounding community and different neighborhood businesses, have students explore various sections of the neighborhood with a family member. Invite a community member to come to the school and share his or her role in the community and ways to support student learning. Provide students with a checklist of places to visit and community members to speak with in order to learn about their roles in the community. Leave room in the checklist for students to add a few places that may be unique to their neighborhoods.
Learning Chess	**Establish Community Chess Mentors:** Learning chess can be a fun and exciting experience, and many schools have chess clubs or use chess playing as an extracurricular activity. If your school doesn't have resources to hire a chess coach or a teacher to lead the club, a creative way to provide an opportunity for students to play with experts is to partner with a community facility for older adults, so that some can serve as coaches and partners. If the older adults aren't able to travel to your school, students can also show them how to use an online chess program and they can play each other remotely. This opportunity would also give the older adults practice with using the computer.

Peg's example illustrates how teachers can "use collaborative tools to expand students' authentic, real-world learning experiences by engaging virtually with experts, teams and students, locally and globally" (ISTE, 2017).

Projects to Encourage Community, Family, and School Collaboration

In this section, we provide sample projects and ideas to engage community members and families with school. We believe children need explicit opportunities to learn about life skills such as kindness and civic responsibility. Creativity and innovation flourish when children are engaged in meaningful, relevant learning experiences.

Random Acts of Kindness Project

This can project can be done with any grade level.

Research with children random acts of kindness and ask them to come up with their own ideas related to this concept (Figure 6.1). Provide the students with hearts on which they write their random acts of kindness ideas and then use the hearts to create a tree in the back of the classroom.

Figure 6.1 This examples shows a Random Acts of Kindness Tree and school-wide collaboration to spread kindness.

The Random Acts of Kindness Foundation (https://randomactsofkindness.org) provides a variety of online resources you can use to support this project.

Here are some more tips for this project:

- Create a class or school wiki page with ideas on how to spread kindness. Ask families to contribute to this wiki page as well.
- Provide students with blank note cards and ask them to write letters of kindness to strangers and leave them around the school and community for others to pick up.
- Become a "RAKtivist" and create a third-party compliments box. Watch this YouTube video "#ThirdPartyCompliments 2015" (https://youtu.be/o-2dGZvN608) for more information on how to simply integrate this in your school, classroom, or community.
- Explore thirteen ways to create a school culture of kindness at the Random Acts of Kindness Foundation site (tinyurl.com/NYI-RAKideas).
- Use the hashtag #thirdpartycompliments on Twitter or Instagram and share your compliments about someone online.

Hosting Community Events with Family, School, and Community

This can be used school-wide, with any grade level.

We recommend bringing the family, school, and community together for events where local community organizations can be present. These events provide stress-free fun for families, schools, and communities and opportunities to connect and build relationships (Figure 6.2). For example, the local police chief attended an event and provided rides in the police car for interested children and allowed them to try on bulletproof vests and handcuffs (Figure 6.3). Public librarians can attend and provide information to families about local and current events. See Figure 6.4 for an example of an invitation to send to community partners about family and community events.

Figure 6.2 Bringing families and the community together through collaboration can provide stress-free fun.

Figure 6.3 The local chief of police attended the family and community event, providing a good opportunity for students and families to engage with community members, like police officers, in a positive way. Photo credit: Sarah Cominskie

RE: Community and Family Event
....

Date of the Event

To Whom It May Concern:

We are planning an event as part of our end-of-year activities. The event will take place at _____ on _____ from 6 to 8 p.m. The purpose of the event is to:

- provide families with ideas on ways to transition over the summer to prevent summer learning loss;
- promote family interaction and raise awareness for community resources;
- bring different families and cultures together; and
- provide literacy for all learners.

We are requesting representatives from community organizations to please join us during the event. If your organization has upcoming events for families, this would be a great opportunity to share this information and provide any materials you may have. If a representative cannot be available, we would like to request information from you that we could please provide to the families who attend. We appreciate any time and/or resources you may be able to offer. Thank you for your consideration.

Sincerely,

Figure 6.4 This letter is an example of an invitation that could be sent to community partners about a family and community event.

Civic Engagement Lesson with Role Play

This project is for use with kindergarten-aged students, but it can be modified for older or younger children.

Laura Tebbens integrates language arts and civic engagement. She encourages creativity by having the children role play how to vote in a teacher-made voting booth (Figure 6.5). After reading the book *Duck for President* by Doreen Cronin, Laura has the children choose their candidate and cast their vote. The full lesson plan can be found on our wiki (goo.gl/agCDgN).

Community Garden Project

This can be used school-wide, with any grade level.

Rashanha and Carey shared the following service-learning project they did with young children. The purpose of their project was "to give back to the community and promote healthy eating." The class planted their own garden with the purpose of donating the food they grew to food banks, families, or shelters in their community.

The project addresses Next Generation Science Standard (NGSS) K-LS1-1: Use observations to describe patterns of what plants and animals (including humans) need to survive.

Rashanha and Carey shared the following tips on implementing this project:

Figure 6.5 Laura Tebbens created a voting booth to go along with her civic engagement lesson. The kindergartners were able to role play and cast their vote for their favorite candidate. Photo credit: Laura Tebbens

- Have children be responsible for all aspects of the garden, including planting, maintaining, and distributing the food that they grow.
- In order to connect to NGSS, have students video or take photographs and voice record their observations of the plants; have them describe how they are taking care of the plants and how the plants grow as a result.
- Have students drop off the food they grow in their gardens to people within the community. For example, have them bring food to homeless shelters, low income families, and retirement homes.
- Ask families to help with transporting the vegetables to the different homeless shelters, low income families, and retirement homes of their choice.

Ways to integrate technology:

- Students can use laptops to research the lifecycle of plants.
- Students can create videos of their plants growing.

- Students can collaborate with other students on the project through apps.

St. Jude Trike-A-Thon

This can be used school-wide, with any grade level.

Marcella and Rob shared a way to engage with the community by participating in the St. Jude Trike-A-Thon. The purpose of the event is to promote bike safety while helping children in need. When asked why they integrate service-learning, they responded, "Service-learning engages students in learning things outside of the classroom and academic setting. Service-learning can expose them to the circumstances of community needs."

Marcella and Rob shared the following ways to engage families, students, and the community:

- Collaborate with St. Jude Children's Research Hospital to get approval from them to host the event.
- Welcome families of the children from St. Jude to join the event as well as involve parents from your school. Encourage families to bring food or drinks to the event and to interact with one another and partake in the races and activities.
- Incorporate the children through a variety of incentives such as prizes, games, and other fun activities at the event. Activities such as trike races, face painting, and carnival games will encourage the children to come to an event that supports a good cause.
- Reach out to local businesses and companies to help promote this event via flyers, posters, internet advertisements, and so on.

Remembering Military Families

This project was submitted by Mary DePaul, MEd, Instructional Technology, and can be used school-wide, with any grade level.

Service-learning is an integral component to my classroom community. In 2016, our class chose a local Army Base, United States Army War College and Carlisle Barracks, to adopt as our service-learning recipients. Adults in the military are often the focus of holiday donations, whereas their kids often are forgotten. Many times, financial woes double the hardships that these children go through in addition to

Figure 6.6 Fifth-grade students took part in service-learning by remembering military families and the hardships they encountered. They donated board games and cards as gifts because those were activities they enjoyed with their own families. Photo credit: Mary DePaul

the separation from loved ones. So, we brainstormed ideas to specifically help the children who may have one, or both, parents deployed at the same time.

My fifth graders chose to focus on fun and cost-effective activities they enjoy with their parents, like playing games and cards and reading (Figure 6.6). The students in my class made posters and spoke to the student body at specific lunch times to ask for donations of new board games and books for the children of servicemen and servicewomen at the base. They collected, organized, and wrapped the board games and gifts, and we delivered them to the children at the base. The class learned so much from this activity: citizenship, public speaking, organization, distribution, and much more. But mostly, the class learned that empathy and kindness feel great.

Ideas for Service-Learning Projects Connected to CCSS

Nicole Draper created the following table (Table 6.1) of ideas on how to implement service-learning in the classroom. Her ideas include curricular objectives, links to Common Core State Standards (CCSS), and guiding questions.

Table 6.1 Ideas for Service Learning Projects by Nicole Draper

Name of Organization	Subject Area	Project Topic/Title	Curricular Goals & Objectives	Guiding Questions	Student Roles
Kind to Kids Foundation: Hope and Help for Children in Need	Math	Operation Kind to Kids	Student use math standards to raise money for materials in order to put together emergency care packages for children. CCSS.Math.Content.2.MD.C.8 Solve word problems involving dollar bills, quarters, dimes, nickels, and pennies, using $ and ¢ symbols appropriately.	What types of materials will be needed? What will we make and sell to earn money for supplies?	Students will organize raising money to provide stuffed animals and fleece blankets for emergency care packages for children entering foster care.
Children and Families First	ELA	Comfort and Compassion	CCSS.ELA-Literacy.W.2.3 Write narratives in which they recount a well-elaborated event or short sequence of events, include details to describe actions, thoughts, and feelings, use temporal words to signal event order, and provide a sense of closure.	How can we offer comfort to those who are going through difficult times? What materials will we need to make our books?	Students will read *A Terrible Thing Happened* by Margaret Holmes and then reflect on it. Students will write a book to distribute to children who are in distress.
Delaware Zoological Society	Science	Save a Species	Students learn and understand that a delicate balance exists within an ecosystem. If there are too many animals for the available resources, some will starve, others move, and some adapt. If there are few animals, the species could become extinct.	Why is it important to save animals? How will we raise the $50 for adopting the class bird?	Students will help save the birds by Adopting a Bird for $50 at their local zoo.

+ Reflection Questions

Here are some questions to consider after you've completed this chapter:

- What issues related to civic engagement have students brought up as important to them?
- What kind of supports will you need from your administrators to create a service-learning experience?
- What tools and technology are available to you?
- How can you use the service-learning experience to build your students' critical-thinking and creativity skills?
- How can you encourage students to work collaboratively to complete the service-learning project?
- How can you or do you involve families and the larger community in service-learning projects with children?
- How can you leverage technology to facilitate the communication between students and the community?
- What one thing will you try after reading this chapter?

Conclusion

Bringing It All Together

"You can't use up creativity. The more you use, the more you have."

— Maya Angelou

As we conclude this book, we want to acknowledge and explain how the contributions of teachers (some we knew and some we connected with through our online survey request) and our students, families, and community members helped to shape our writing and motivate us to continue exploring how we can best foster innovation and creativity in our youngest learners. Before we started this book, we understood how critical the connection is between the school, family, and the community in relation to a child's development and growth, and we were passionate about nurturing young children to be innovators and creators. What we didn't realize was how much excitement and support we would receive from our many contributors. We requested stories through social media such as Twitter, Facebook, and LinkedIn, and we reached out personally to co-workers and students (past and present) who we knew had ideas related to this topic that they could share and from which others could benefit. We had conversations at social events, in our offices, and in our own classrooms about our book and the information we were seeking. We believe that all of our knowledge and experience related to working with children and adults told us that we needed more than just our own ideas to make this book relevant and useful. Receiving stories and having conversations with others helped us to think and dig deeper into topics we may not have even considered.

The most surprising part of this process was receiving stories from unexpected places. The Community Connections section of each chapter came about from receiving diverse responses from community members that we felt would be beneficial to others. For example, a neighbor down the street saw our request on Twitter, and shared how he worked through his company with the local high school to teach innovation skills and Systematic Inventive Thinking. Also, a childhood friend, who now lives 3,000 miles away, saw our request on Facebook, and sent a picture of his daughter and shared the story of a STEAM project they had created together. And, after having a conversation with a family member about creating trauma-sensitive environments, we realized how important doing this is for creating an atmosphere that fosters innovation and creativity. The process of requesting the stories helped us to be more creative and innovative with the direction of our writing and it helped demonstrate why teachers, families, and community members need opportunities to discuss, share, and innovate together.

As important as it is for us all to nurture young learners, we need to nurture our own creativity and innovation by opening ourselves up to others' perspectives, ideas, and stories. We never know where our ideas may come from and what we might learn. If we create an environment that allows for curiosity and questions and exploration for ourselves, it will be easier for us to do this for the learners and families we meet along the way. Schools can help by hosting events that bring the families and communities together. In addition, teachers need opportunities to talk with one another and to know they can try things out in their classrooms and take risks. There needs to be a culture of risk-taking and learning from mistakes to make allowances for when things do not go as we had planned. Communities can help by hosting events that bring the schools and families together and families can help by being open to ideas and working with schools and communities. We, as teacher educators and researchers, can help by continuing to share stories and engage current and future teachers in innovative and creative activities, and stressing the importance of making these connections between home, school, and community.

In our introduction, we mentioned that we would provide ideas within the book aligned with the U.S. Department of Education and the U.S. Department of Health and Human Services (2016) policy on early learning and educational technology, which has provided four guiding principles related to the use of technology with early learners:

- Guiding Principle #1: Technology—when used appropriately—can be a tool for learning.

- Guiding Principle #2: Technology should be used to increase access to learning opportunities for all children.
- Guiding Principle #3: Technology may be used to strengthen relationships among parents, families, early educators, and young children.
- Guiding Principle #4: Technology is more effective for learning when adults and peers interact or co-view with young children. (p. 7)

We hope that what we have shared will assist those working with young learners to meet these four guiding principles so that young children can grow and develop with the use of technology and that technology is used appropriately. Throughout the book, we stressed the importance of focusing on the learning, and not the tool. Although we shared specific examples of tools that can be used, we know there are too many tools to mention all of them (and new ones come out every day). We continue to stress the importance of focusing on learning over the tool.

Within each chapter, we focused on at least one ISTE Student Standard and found this helped us to consider the important skills and abilities learners need to thrive in a global and digital society. The Student Standards complemented our book and the ideas we had as they focus on a student-driven environment that fosters innovation, creativity, communication, and collaboration, as well as empowering students to use technology to redefine their learning.

We invite you to continue the conversation with us and share your stories through our online Google Forms survey (tinyurl.com/InnovationandCreativityISTE).

We hope you can use the many tips, exercises, and suggested projects we provided throughout the book. As a reminder, the exercises can also be downloaded for your use from our Nurturing Young Innovators wiki (https://nurturingyounginnovators .wikispaces.com).

You can also use a QR scanner and scan this QR code to access our wiki:

Thank you again to all of our contributors who shared their pictures, stories, and passion for nurturing young innovators and cultivating creativity in the classroom, home, and community. We know this collaborative effort made our book better and more useful for anyone looking for ideas and suggestions on fostering innovation and creativity in the lives of young learners.

Appendix A

Resources and Tools for Nurturing Young Innovators

We have referenced many websites, books, articles, and technology tools throughout this book. In this section, we've collected those resources and also added a variety of additional ones that can be used to support your work in nurturing young innovators. We hope that you find these resources useful.

Chapter 1 Resources

In Chapter 1, we discuss ways teachers can nurture young innovators by incorporating creativity, innovation, and technology integration in the early years. Here are some additional resources that can be leveraged to build a toolkit for helping students to grow as digital citizens and innovative designers.

Common Sense Media (https://www.commonsensemedia.org)

- How to Choose the Right Apps for Your Kids (goo.gl/zH9GhA)
- Essential Creativity Guide (goo.gl/tajZ0y)
- Setting Screen-Time Limits (goo.gl/5GkxCU)
- Digital Citizenship iBook Lessons (goo.gl/GzkEBR)
- Best Games and Websites for Teaching Critical Thinking, Creativity, Communication, and Collaboration (goo.gl/Rwx0Gn)
- Top Tech Tools for Formative Assessment (goo.gl/TZCZFv)

Other Resources

- Inside the Box (www.insidetheboxinnovation.com/resources) – Learn about innovation and systematic inventing thinking
- GoNoodle (https://www.gonoodle.com) – A great place to find ideas for movement and brain breaks

- The Learning Station's YouTube channel (https://youtu.be/388Q44Re OWE) – Videos for brain breaks

The Fred Rogers Center (fredrogerscenter.org)

- Digital Media and Learning Resources (goo.gl/Bn4s2s)
- Checklist for Assessing Technology Integration from The Pennsylvania Digital Media Literacy Project (goo.gl/t2CK4m)
- Ten Questions for Educators to Ask When Using Technology with Young Children (goo.gl/vsdLH7)

Twitter Hashtags to Follow

- #elemmathtalk
- #brainbreaks
- #creativeplay
- #digitalequity
- #GlobalEDchat
- #innovativedesigner
- #theglobaleducator
- #nurturingyounginnovators

Twitter Feeds to Follow

- @FredRogersCtr – The latest Tweets from the Fred Rogers Center, which helps children grow as confident, competent, and caring human beings
- @Common Sense – Advice for families about technology and apps to use with young children
- @GoNoodle – Ideas on how to engage children with brain breaks
- @DrewBoyd – An expert on Systematic Inventive Thinking and Inside the Box innovation
- @ISTEconnects – The latest Tweets from the International Society for Technology in Education (ISTE)

Ch 2 Resources

In Chapter 2, we build on the resources that can support creativity and innovation in young children and encourage them to start to take risks. To assist you as you continue to encourage young innovators, we have listed a variety of resources for risk-taking. We have included resources on how to get the family involved with math and supports for stress-free math activities, as math is part of STEAM (science, technology, engineering, the arts, and math), which we discuss in Chapter 5.

Resources on Risk-Taking

- *Audri's Rube Goldberg Monster Trap* on YouTube (https://youtu.be/0uDD EEHDf1Y) – A great video for encouraging risk-taking
- "Early Childhood Risk Taking" Pinterest board (www.pinterest.com/ exearlylearning/early-childhood-risk-taking)

Family Resources Related to Math

- Figure This! Math Challenges for Families (figurethis.nctm.org)
- Family Math Night Resources (familymathnight.com/resources)
- Lori Lite's Stress Free Kids: Making Math Fun (https://stressfreekids .com/14688/making-math-fun)

Trauma-Sensitive Resources

- The Trauma and Learning Policy Initiative (TLPI) (https://trauma sensitiveschools.org) – A collaboration of Massachusetts Advocates for Children and Harvard Law School
- Delaware Department of Education: Trauma-Informed Practices and Compassionate Schools Model Information (www.doe.k12.de.us/ domain/240)

Twitter Hashtags to Follow

- #edchat
- #edtech
- #risktaking
- #traumasensitive
- #ACEs
- #traumainformed

Twitter Feeds to Follow

- @TEC_Center – Resources about the appropriate use of technology in the early years
- @ECEtech – Tips from the Early Childhood Technology Network on appropriate apps, technology, and websites
- @geniushour – A dedicated time for students to explore their passions

Chapter 3 Resources

We hope that Chapter 3 has inspired you to include your students' families in all aspects of nurturing their young innovators. Here are links to blogs and organizations that provide ideas on engaging families in the work of nurturing the creativity of young learners. We also suggest resources for effectively using technology to communicate with families and resources for providing supports for families in crisis.

Resources to Engage Families in Nurturing Young Learners

- Bruce VanPatter: Ideas for Families (www.brucevanpatter.com/family ideas.html) – Activities to spark creativity in young learners
- National Association for the Education of Young Children (NAEYC): Using Technology to Engage Families (www.naeyc.org/tyc/10x-using -technology)
- Digital Promise: Using Technology for Effective Parent-Teacher Communication (digitalpromise.org/2014/09/17/using-technology-for -effective-parent-teacher-communication)
- Knapp Elementary School: Family Engagement Wiki (knappwiki.wiki spaces.com)
- Fractus Learning: Using Technology to Enhance Communication with Families and the School Community (https://www.fractuslearning.com/ 2014/05/27/communication-families-school)
- Table Talk Math (tabletalkmath.com) – A great resource for talking to kids about math

Resources to Support Families

- Families in Crisis, Inc. (familiesincrisis.org) – An organization that provides support for families who are affected by incarceration or the criminal justice system
- Child Welfare Information Gateway (https://www.childwelfare.gov) – Resources related to child welfare, child abuse and neglect, adoption, and immigration support
- The Learning Community: Tips for Parents: Immigrant Families (www.thelearningcommunity.us/resources-by-format/tips-for-parents/ diverse-families/immigrant-families.aspx) – Tips for parents on education, finding a home, and making a living
- American Psychological Association: Caring for Chronically Ill Kids (www.apa.org/monitor/2011/03/ill-children.aspx)

- Global Partnership for Education: Children with Disabilities (global-partnership.org/focus-areas/children-with-disabilities) – Information on how to best support families/children with disabilities
- Family Promise (familypromise.org) – Resources and services for homeless families and those at-risk for being homeless

Twitter Hashtags to Follow

- #familiesincrisis
- #WiFionwheels

Twitter Feeds to Follow

- @NAEYC – Expert advice for families and educators working with young children
- @APA – Resources from the American Psychological Association to help families and educators working with young learners
- @ChildWelfareGov – Information for helping support families and children
- @GPforEducation – Global Partnership for Education, supporting more than 60 countries to ensure children receive quality education

Chapter 4 Resources

In Chapter 4, we stress the value of providing choice to young children. Here are some additional resources to help support families, differentiate learning, and allow choice in young learners.

- RTI Action Network: Engaging Families in Early Childhood Education (rtinetwork.org/essential/family/engagingfamilies)
- Collaborative Genius Hour Wikispace (geniushour.wikispaces.com)
- Dare to Differentiate Wikispace (https://daretodifferentiate.wikispaces .com/Choice+Boards) – Many ideas for choice boards and differentiation strategies
- Project Appleseed: Benefits & Barriers to Family Involvement in Education (projectappleseed.org/barriers)
- Clemson University Extension Family and Consumer Sciences: Building Family Strengths (clemson.edu/fyd/bfs.htm)
- Epstein's Framework of Six Types of Involvement (https://www.gpo.gov/ fdsys/pkg/ERIC-ED467082/pdf/ERIC-ED467082.pdf)

- Harvard Family Research Project: The Family Involvement Network of Educators (hfrp.org/family-involvement/fine-family-involvement-network-of-educators)
- John Hopkins University: National Network of Partnership Schools (nnps.jhucsos.com)
- Parents as Teachers (parentsasteachers.org)

Twitter Hashtags to Follow

- #activelearning
- #flexibleseating
- #geniushour
- #GrowthMindset
- #UDLchat
- #universaldesignforlearning

Twitter Feeds to Follow

- @parentsasteachers – An evidenced-based home visiting model and a variety of parent education and family support curricula
- @UDL_Center – Many ideas on the use of Universal Design for Learning
- @UMD_FamilyLab – Family involvement laboratory at the University of Maryland, directed by Natasha Cabrera, Ph.D.

Chapter 5 Resources

In Chapter 5, we share many ways to make, create, and innovate with early learners to encourage creativity in the classroom, home, and community. Here we share some additional resources specific for integrating STEAM and makerspaces with your own students, including interesting and helpful Twitter feeds and handles related to this topic.

- Pretty Brainy: Empowering Girls to Gain STEAM: STEM to STEAM (https://prettybrainy.com/girls-in-stem-steam-learning)
- EdSurge: The Importance of Maker Education for Girls (https://www.edsurge.com/news/2015-05-24-the-importance-of-maker-education-for-girls)
- FabLearn at Stanford Graduate School of Education: *Meaningful Making: Projects and Inspiration for Fab Labs and Makerspaces* Edited by Paulo Blikstein, Sylvia Libow Martinez, and Heather Allen Pang (goo.gl/YQV8pE)

Twitter Hashtags to Follow

- #codingforkids
- #girlswhocode
- #hourofcode
- #STEAMmaker
- #engineeringrocks

Twitter Feeds to Follow

- Best Colleges Online: 50 Essential Twitter Feeds for STEM Educators (linkis.com/com/DZjvr)
- @codeorg – A nonprofit exposing students to coding and computer science
- @MakerEdOrg – Ideas on how to incorporate making with young children
- @Makerready – Helps schools become maker schools
- @Makerspaces_com – Resources on how to implement makerspaces in your school or library
- @DiscoveryGV – Discovery Teacher, Mr. Creed, who shared about fairy tale engineering

Chapter 6 Resources

Community-based activities can encourage young learners to explore meaningful real-life situations where they learn how to problem solve and think critically. For this reason, in Chapter 6, we provide ideas on how to integrate service-learning and community-based projects with young learners. Here are some additional resources to extend this support.

- The Center for the Study of Social Policy: *The Strengthening Families Approach and Protective Factors Framework: Branching Out and Reaching Deeper* by Charlyn Harper Browne (goo.gl/fxztvq)
- Children's Defense Fund (childrensdefense.org)
- Families and Work Institute: *2014 National Study of Employers* by Kenneth Matos and Ellen Galinsky (familiesandwork.org/downloads/2014NationalStudyOfEmployers.pdf)
- Families and Work Institute (familiesandwork.org)
- Ohio Department of Education: Framework for Building Partnerships Among Schools, Families and Communities (goo.gl/CZtjOJ)

- We Are Teachers: 3 STEAM Projects That Build a Better Tomorrow (https://www.weareteachers.com/3-steam-projects-that-build-a-better-tomorrow)

Twitter Hashtags to Follow

- #servicelearning
- #pbl
- #childrensdefensefund
- #familyengagement
- #communityengagement

Twitter Feeds to Follow

- @BIEpbl – Ideas related to project-based learning from Bucks Institute for Education
- @FWInews – The latest Tweets from the Families and Work Institute, which provides research related to families and work
- @YouthService – Service ideas from Youth Service America, which helps youth ages 5 to 25 find their voice to advocate and take action to help others
- @ChildDefender – The latest Tweets from The Children's Defense Fund, a nonprofit focusing on child advocacy that has been leveling the playing field for all children since 1973

Other Resources

Here are two additional resources to help educators support and nurture young innovators. The first is a list of technology competencies that we developed—based on the guidelines from the Office of Educational Technology—for university professors, preservice teachers, and classroom teachers to use to self-assess their own use of technology. The second is a guide we created (Exercise A.1) for educators to use to reflect on their use of technology in the classroom.

Competencies for University Professors, Preservice Teachers, and Classroom Teachers to Demonstrate Proficiency in Technology Use

The Office of Educational Technology (n.d.) recommended that teacher education programs develop a set of technology competency expectations for university professors and preservice teachers exiting a teacher education program that demonstrate they are proficient in technology use and integration. Using the roles and practices the Office of Educational Technology has developed for teachers, we came up with the following guidelines that can be used to help university professors and future teachers determine whether they are proficient in the area of technology use and create an action plan for the areas that they may want to develop and concentrate on.

Competency #1: Educators demonstrate proficiency in technology use when they collaborate with one another and share their expertise beyond the walls of the university or school.

Suggested ways to demonstrate proficiency in this competency:

- Publications on the topic
- Presentations on the topic
- Projects completed with other educators
- Self-reflection that includes specific ways you collaborated and shared your expertise beyond the walls of the university or school

Competency #2: Educators demonstrate proficiency in technology use by designing highly engaging and relevant learning experiences.

Suggested ways to demonstrate proficiency in this competency:

- Peer, dean, and supervisor observations
- Self-assessment identifying technology use and learning experiences
- Sharing lesson plans and assessments that integrate technology
- Videos, pictures, and so on

Competency #3: Educators demonstrate proficiency in technology use when they lead the evaluation and implementation of new technologies for learning.

Suggested ways to demonstrate proficiency in this competency:

- Peer, dean, and supervisor observations
- Self-assessment identifying technology use and learning experiences
- Sharing lesson plans and assessments that integrate technology
- Videos, pictures, and so on

Competency #4: Educators demonstrate proficiency in technology use when they serve as guides, facilitators, and motivators for learners.

Suggested ways to demonstrate proficiency in this competency:

- Peer, dean, and supervisor observations
- Self-assessment identifying technology use and learning experiences
- Sharing lesson plans and assessments that integrate technology
- Videos, pictures, and so on

Competency #5: Educators demonstrate proficiency to technology use by being co-learners with students and peers.

Suggested ways to demonstrate proficiency in this competency:

- Peer, dean, and supervisor observations
- Self-assessment identifying technology use and learning experiences
- Sharing lesson plans and assessments that integrate technology
- Videos, pictures, and so on

Competency #6: Educators demonstrate proficiency in technology use by becoming a catalyst to serve the underserved.

Suggested ways to demonstrate proficiency in this competency:

- Documentation of how you advocated for those who did not have equal access to technology
- Sharing ideas and tools on how to level the playing field when it comes to technology use
- Obtaining grants to fund initiatives to serve the underserved
- Sharing lesson plans and assessments demonstrating ways to serve all learners

Assessing Technology Use with Early Learners

The Assessing Technology Use with Early Learners exercise (Exercise A.1) can be used to help adults assess the learning outcomes and the use of technology with early learners. It can be completed as part of a course assignment and/or professional development/learning community. We provide a template of this document on our wiki.

» Exercise A.1 Assessing Technology Use with Early Learners

Name of the technology/tool:

Description of the technology:

What learning outcomes are you focusing on for young learners? Please list any state or national standards if applicable.

Is this technology developmentally appropriate for this group of children and/or individual child? Is it individually appropriate? Is it culturally appropriate? Is it age appropriate?

Please explain why the technology is or is not developmentally appropriate:

In what ways (other than the use of technology) have the learning outcomes noted above been addressed within your classroom?

Please describe how the use of this technology helps students develop one of the 4Cs (creativity, critical thinking, collaboration, and communication). Please be specific:

Appendix B

References

ACE Response. (2017). *ACEs in education.* Retrieved from www.aceresponse.org/give_ your_support/ACEs-in-Education_25_68_sb.htm

Almon, J. (2013, August 20). *The role of risk in play and learning.* Retrieved from Community Playthings website: www.communityplaythings.com/resources/articles/2013/ the-role-of-risk-in-play-and-learning

Anderson, M., & Perrin, A. (2016, September 7). *13% of Americans don't use the internet. Who are they?* Retrieved from Pew Research Center website: www.pewresearch.org/ fact-tank/2016/09/07/some-americans-dont-use-the-internet-who-are-they

Apodaca, A. (2017). Makerspace next. *CSLA Journal, 40*(2), 5–8.

Association of American Colleges and Universities. (2007). *Top ten things employers look for in new college graduates.* Retrieved from www.aacu.org/leap/students/employers -top-ten

Association of Experiential Education. (n.d.). *What is experiential education?* Retrieved from www.aee.org/what-is-ee

Boone, M., Hendricks, M., & Waller, R. (2014). Closing the digital divide and its impact on minorities. *The Global eLearning Journal, 3*(1), 1–6. Retrieved from https://globale learningjournal.files.wordpress.com/2010/11/closing-the-digital-divide-geljvol3i1.pdf

Boyd, D. (2015, March 2). The creative power of children. Systematic creativity is a skill that even children can learn. *Psychology Today.* Retrieved from https://www .psychologytoday.com/blog/inside-the-box/201503/the-creative-power-children

Boyd, D., & Goldenberg, J. (2013). *Inside the box. A proven system of creativity for break- through results.* New York, NY: Simon & Schuster.

Boyle, J., Butler, M., & Li, J. (2017). Thinking, not stuff: Re-imagining young children's engagement with technology and innovation. In Chip Donahue (Ed.), *Family engage- ment in the digital age.* (pp. 41–57). New York, NY: Routledge.

Buck Institute for Education (BIE). (2017). *What is project-based learning (PBL)?* Retrieved from www.bie.org/about/what_pbl

Budhai, S., & Taddei, L. (2015). *Teaching the 4cs with technology: How do I use 21st century tools to teach 21st century skills?* Alexandria, VA: ASCD Arias.

Carroll, K. (2012, July 27). *Play is necessary: Kevin Carroll at TEDxHarlem* [Video file]. Retrieved from https://youtu.be/1pz72Wygg8c

Centers for Disease Control and Prevention (2012). Engaging parents. https://www.cdc.gov/healthyyouth/protective/parent_engagement.htm

The Centre for Research in Education and Educational Technology. (n.d.). Possibility thinking. Retrieved from The Open University website: www.open.ac.uk/creet/main/sites/www.open.ac.uk.creet.main/files/06%20Possibility%20Thinking.pdf

Coates, K. (2013, September 28). Nurturing a growth mindset in early learners: Part II [Blog post]. Retrieved from http://blog.mindsetworks.com/entry/nurturing-a-growth-mindset-in-early-learners

Common Core State Standards Initiative (2017). Read the standards. www.corestandards.org/read-the-standards

Connell, G. (2016, January 6). Setting (almost) SMART goals with my students [Blog post]. Retrieved from https://www.scholastic.com/teachers/blog-posts/genia-connell/setting-almost-smart-goals-my-students

Couchenour, D., & Chrisman, K. (2014). *Families, schools and communities. Together for young children* (5th ed.). Belmont, CA: Wadsworth.

Defors, J. (2016, December 1). *Encouraging student risk-taking by grading the process not the product.* Retrieved from Center Cass School District website: www.ccsd66.org/encouraging-student-risk-taking-by-grading-the-process-not-the-product

Delzer, K. (2016, April 22). Flexible seating and student-centered classroom redesign [Blog post]. Retrieved from https://www.edutopia.org/blog/flexible-seating-student-centered-classroom-kayla-delzer

Dewey, J. (1938). *Experience and education.* New York, NY: Macmillan.

Digital Citizenship: It's not just good curriculum, it's the law. (2016). *T H E Journal, 43*(6), 22.

Duncan, S., & Salcedo, M. (2015, January/February). Are your children in Times Square? Moving from confinement to engagement. *Exchange, 221,* 26–29.

Dweck, C. (2014). *The power of believing that you can improve* [Video file]. Retrieved from the TED website: https://www.ted.com/talks/carol_dweck_the_power_of_believing_that_you_can_improve?utm_source=tedcomshare&utm_medium=referral&utm_campaign=tedspread

Epstein, J. L., Jansorn, N. R., Salinas, K. C., Sanders, M. G., Simon, B. S., & Van Voorhis, F. L. (2002). *School, family, and community partnerships: Your handbook for action.* Thousand Oaks, CA: Corwin Press. Retrieved from https://www.gpo.gov/fdsys/pkg/ERIC-ED467082/pdf/ERIC-ED467082.pdf

Finley, K. (2014, October 24). *4 ways to encourage a growth mindset in the classroom.* Retrieved from EdSurge website: https://www.edsurge.com/news/2014-10-24-4-ways-to-encourage-a-growth-mindset-in-the-classroom

Garcia, L., & Thornton, O. (2014). The enduring importance of parental involvement. *neaToday.* http://neatoday.org/2014/11/18/the-enduring-importance-of-parental-involvement-2

Gray, P. (2014). *The decline of play: Peter Gray at TEDxNavesink* [Video file]. Retrieved from the TED website: http://ed.ted.com/on/bt6AeE9S

Grossman, S. (n.d.). Offering children choices: Encouraging autonomy and learning while minimizing conflicts. *Early Childhood News.* Retrieved from www.earlychildhoodnews.com/earlychildhood/article_view.aspx?ArticleID=607

Harte, H. A. (2013). Universal design and outdoor learning. *Dimensions of Early Childhood, 41*(3), 18–22.

Heraper, S. (2017). The philosophy of makerspaces. *CSLA Journal, 40*(2), 3–9.

Herczog, M. M. (2016). Next generation citizens: Promoting civic engagement in schools. *Leadership, 45*(5), 24–28.

Herold, C. (2010). *Let's raise kids to be entrepreneurs* [Video file]. Retrieved from the TED website: https://www.ted.com/talks/cameron_herold_let_s_raise_kids_to_be_entrepreneurs?utm_source=tedcomshare&utm_medium=referral&utm_campaign=tedspread

Hummell, L. H. (2015). Curiosity and inquiry. *Children's Technology & Engineering, 19*(3), 5–6.

Instructables (n.d). Instructables.com/id/Make-a-Vibrobot

International Society for Technology in Education (2016). ISTE Standards for Students. Retrieved from https://www.iste.org/standards/standards/for-students

International Society for Technology in Education (2017). ISTE Standards for Educators. https://www.iste.org/standards

Isenberg, J., & Jalongo, M. (2014). *Creative thinking and arts-based learning: Preschool through fourth grade* (6th ed.). Upper Saddle River, NJ: Pearson.

Jacoby, B. (1999). Partnerships for service learning. *New Directions for Student Services, 87,* 18–35.

Jarrett, K. (2016). Makerspaces and design thinking: Perfect together! *Education Digest, 82*(4), 50–54.

Kessler, C. (2013). *What is genius hour?* Retrieved from the Genius Hour website: www.geniushour.com/what-is-genius-hour

Kim, H. J., Park, J. H., Yoo, S., & Kim, H. (2016). Fostering creativity in tablet-based interactive classrooms. *Educational Technology & Society, 19*(3), 207–220.

Kinnard, M. (2017, March 20). Wi-fi on wheels. Google helps students get online, on the go. Retrieved from AP: The Big Story website: bigstory.ap.org/article/5f394f60d0344748bb4f9be0579bc762/wi-fi-wheels-google-helps-students-get-online-go

Kyritsis, E. (2014). Genius hour. [Blog post]. Retrieved from https://elenikyritsis.com/2014/08/27/genius-hour

Lacey, R. (2017). A surplus of soft skills. Educators find an ideal approach to teaching problem-solving, creativity, teamwork, and grit. *District Administration (Special Report, Makerspaces: Meeting of the Mindsets), 23–26.* Retrieved from www.nxtbook.com/pmg/DA/DA_SR0117Final/index.php?device=cpa#/5/OnePage

Letter, T. (2016, May 23). Ignite student passion with genius hour [Blog post]. Retrieved from https://www.commonsense.org/education/blog/ignite-student-passions-with-genius-hour

Levin-Goldberg, J. (2009, September/October). Five ways to increase civic engagement. *Social Studies and the Young Learner, 22*(1), 15–18. Retrieved from www.socialstudies.org/publications/ssyl/september-october2009/five_ways_to_increase_civic_engagement

Levitt, T. (2002, August). Creativity is not enough. *Harvard Business Review.* Retrieved from https://hbr.org/2002/08/creativity-is-not-enough

Lynch, M. (2017, February 4). *Why makerspaces are the key to innovation.* Retrieved from The Edvocate website: www.theedadvocate.org/why-makerspaces-are-the-key-to-innovation

Maslyk, J. (2016). *STEAM makers: Fostering creativity and innovation in the elementary classroom.* Thousand Oaks, CA: Corwin.

Matteson, A. (2016). It's genius. *School Library Journal, 62*(10), 36–38.

McCrea, A. B. (2015). A learning transformation guided by teachers. *T H E Journal, 42*(6), 8–12.

MCP Staff. (2017). The importance of play and experiential learning in early childhood [Blog post]. Retrieved from https://www.melbournechildpsychology.com.au/blog/play-experiential-learning-early-childhood

Mitchell, S., Foulger, T., & Wetzel, K. (2009, September). Ten tips for involving families through internet-based communication. *Young Children.* Retrieved from www.naeyc.org/files/yc/file/200909/Ten%20Tips%20for%20Involving%20Families.pdf

National Association for the Education of Young Children. (2016). *Selected examples of effective classroom practice involving technology tools and interactive media.* Retrieved from www.naeyc.org/files/naeyc/PS_technology_Examples.pdf

National Association for the Education of Young Children, & Fred Rogers Center for Early Learning and Children's Media. (2012, January). *Technology and interactive media as tools in early childhood programs serving children from birth through age 8* [Position statement]. Retrieved from www.naeyc.org/files/naeyc/file/positions/PS_technology_ WEB2.pdf

National Center on Universal Design for Learning. (2011). Checkpoint 7.1: Optimize individual choice and autonomy. In *UDL Guidelines—Version 2.0: Examples and Resources*. Retrieved from www.udlcenter.org/implementation/examples/examples7_1

National Cyber Security Alliance: Stay Safe Online. (2017). *Raising digital citizens. Teach your children to become good digital citizens with these resources*. Retrieved from https://staysafeonline.org/stay-safe-online/for-parents/raising-digital-citizens

National Science Teachers Association. (2009, April). *Parent involvement in science education* [Position statement]. Retrieved from www.nsta.org/about/positions/parents.aspx

Next Generation Science Standards: For States, By States. Retrieved from https://www.nextgenscience.org/topic-arrangement/1waves-light-and-sound

NYU Steinhardt School of Culture, Education, and Human Development. (2017). *Study finds play and cognitive skills in kindergarten predict civic engagement in later life*. Retrieved from http://steinhardt.nyu.edu/site/ataglance/2017/01/study-finds-play-and-cognitive-skills-in-kindergarten-predict-civic-engagement-in-later-life.html

Office of Educational Technology. (n.d.). *Call to action* [Brief]. Retrieved from https://tech.ed.gov/earlylearning/calltoaction

Partnership for 21st Century Learning. (2016, January). *Framework for 21st century learning*. Retrieved from www.p21.org/our-work/p21-framework

Partnership for 21st Century Learning. (2015, May). *P21 framework definitions*. Retrieved from www.p21.org/storage/documents/docs/P21_Framework_Definitions_New_ Logo_2015.pdf

Primary Professional Development Services. (n.d.). Differentiation in action! Retrieved from www.pdst.ie/sites/default/files/Session%202%20-%20Differentiation%20 Resource%20_0_0.pdf

Puentedura, R. (2009, February 4). As we may teach. Educational technology, from theory to practice [Blog post]. Retrieved from www.hippasus.com/rrpweblog/ archives/000025.html

Rendina, D. (2015, June 29). Makerspaces in school: Creating STEAM connections [Blog post]. Retrieved from http://ideas.demco.com/blog/makerspaces-in-schools

Reynolds, E. (n.d.). Watch me fly! I'm Superman! *Early Childhood News*. Retrieved from www.earlychildhoodnews.com/earlychildhood/article_view.aspx?ArticleID=111

Rich, M., & Lavallee, K. (2017). The mediatrician's advice for today's media mentors. In Chip Donahue (Ed.), *Family Engagement in the Digital Age*. (pp. 147–160). New York, NY: Routledge.

Schlechty, P. (1994, January). *Increasing student engagement*. Missouri Leadership Academy.

Schrock, A. (2014). "Education in disguise." Culture of a hacker and maker space. *InterActions: UCLA Journal of Education and Information Studies, 10*(1), 1–25.

Schrock, K. (2013, November 9). *SAMR model and Bloom's taxonomy.* Retrieved from Kathy Schrock's Guide to Everything website: www.schrockguide.net/samr.html

Skillicorn, N. (2016, March 9). What is innovation? 15 experts share their innovation definition. Retrieved from the Idea to Value website: https://www.ideatovalue.com/inno/nickskillicorn/2016/03/innovation-15-experts-share-innovation-definition/#petef

Souers, K., & Hall, P. (2016). *Fostering resilient learners: Strategies for creating a trauma-sensitive classroom.* Alexandria, VA: ASCD.

Statman-Weil, K. (2015, May). Creating trauma-sensitive classrooms. *Young Children, (70)*2, 72–79. Retrieved from www.naeyc.org/yc/files/yc/file/201505/YC0515_Trauma-Sensitive_Classrooms_Statman-Weil.pdf

Strimel, G. (2014). Authentic education. *Technology and Engineering Teacher, 73*(7), 8–18.

Sullivan, A., & Bers, M. (2016). Robotics in the early childhood classroom: Learning outcomes from an 8-week robotics curriculum in pre-kindergarten through second grade. *International Journal of Technology & Design Education, 26*(1), 3–20. doi:10.1007/s10798-015-9304-5

Tesconi, S. (2016). Documenting a project using a "failures box." In Paolo Blikstein, Sylvia Libow Martinez, and Heather Allen Pang (Eds.), *Meaningful Making: Projects and Inspirations for Fab Labs and Makerspaces.* (pp. 36). Constructing Modern Knowledge Press.

Thompson, M., & Beymer, P. (2015). The effects of choice in the classroom: Is there too little or too much choice? *Support for Learning, 30*(2), 105–120. doi:10.1111/1467-9604.12086

Thornton, M. (2015, August 31). Creating space for risk [Blog post]. Retrieved from https://www.edutopia.org/blog/creating-space-for-risk-michael-thornton-cheryl-harris

U.S. Department of Education and Office of Educational Technology (2017). Reimagining the Role of Technology in Education: 2017 National Education Technology Plan Update. Retrieved from https://tech.ed.gov/files/2017/01/NETP17.pdf

U.S. Department of Education and U.S. Department of Health and Human Services. (2016, October). *Early learning and educational technology policy brief* [Brief]. Retrieved from https://tech.ed.gov/files/2016/10/Early-Learning-Tech-Policy-Brief.pdf

Vaidyanathan, S. (2012). Fostering creativity and innovation through technology. *Learning and Leading with Technology, 39*(6), 24–27.

Voice of Play (n.d.). *How playtime reduces stress.* Retrieved from Voice of Play website: voiceofplay.org/blog/playtime-reduces-stress

Whitaker, T., Zoul, J., & Casas, J. (2015). *What connected educators do differently.* New York, NY: Routledge.

Yongpradit, P. (2017). Computer science: A playground for 21st century skills. Retrieved from www.p21.org/news-events/p21blog/2128

Index